HELL: THE LOGIC OF DAMNATION

Library of Religious Philosophy
Volume 9

HELL
The Logic of Damnation

JERRY L. WALLS

UNIVERSITY OF NOTRE DAME PRESS
NOTRE DAME   LONDON

Library of Congress Cataloging-in-Publication Data

Walls, Jerry L.
  Hell : the logic of damnation / Jerry L. Walls.
    p. cm. — (Library of religious philosophy ;
    v. 9)
  Includes bibliographical references and index.
  ISBN 0-268-01095-1
  1. Hell—Christianity. I. Title. II. Series.
BT836.2.W33   1992
236'.25—dc20   91-50568
                                        CIP

To Angela Rose
and
Jonathan Levi

CONTENTS

Introduction   1

1. Hell and Human Belief   17

2. Hell and Divine Knowledge   33

3. Hell and Divine Power   57

4. Hell and Divine Goodness   83

5. Hell and Human Freedom   113

6. Hell and Human Misery   139

   Conclusion   157

   Notes   161

   Index   179

ACKNOWLEDGMENTS

Much of the material in Chapter Three appeared earlier in *Scottish Journal of Theology* 38, no. 2 (1985): 155-172. It is used here with the permission of the publisher, Scottish Academic Press. A large portion of Chapter Four was published in *Faith and Philosophy* 7, no. 1 (1990): 85-98. It is reprinted here by the permission of the editors.

Several persons read earlier versions of this material and offered perceptive comments. These include William Abraham, Thomas Flint, Alvin Plantinga, Philip Quinn, and Carole Roos. Others who have discussed my ideas and pushed me to clarify them include David Lutz, John Walls, Patrick Wilson and my colleagues at Asbury, Michael Peterson and Laurence Wood. I must also mention Fred Freddoso, whose seminar on Molina was an important source of stimulus for my thinking on many of these issues. A special word of thanks goes to Tom Morris, whose criticism, advice and encouragement has been invaluable.

During much of my research, I had the benefit of financial support from A Foundation for Theological Education. I am grateful for this assistance, as well as the moral support of A.F.T.E.'s former chariman, Dr. Edmund W. Robb, Jr.

Finally, I am happy to record my appreciation for my wife Patricia and my children Angela and Jonathan, who provided me with a welcome point of contrast during the time I have spent thinking about hell.

INTRODUCTION

I

One of the most famous speeches of all time is a sermon about hell, namely, "Sinners in the Hands of an Angry God" by Jonathan Edwards. Its fame is due largely to its literary qualities, particularly its graphic language.[1] It is rich with passages like the following.

> That world of misery, that lake of burning brimstone is extended abroad under you. *There* is the dreadful pit of the glowing flames of the wrath of God; there is Hell's wide gaping mouth open; and you have nothing to stand upon, nor any thing to take hold of; there is nothing between you and Hell but the air; tis only the power and mere pleasure of God that holds you up.

Countless students of American literature have experienced, through Edwards's sermon "as vivid a glimpse into Hell as the imagination of man has been able to conceive."[2]

The sermon is also noteworthy because of the impact it had on those who originally heard it. As Edwards enlarged on God's wrath and the precarious position of sinners on the brink of hell, his congregation was visibly affected. Many persons cried out, sensing that they were right then slipping to their doom. At one point, the cries were so loud that Edwards had to pause before going on with his sermon. And this took place, we recall, not at a wilderness tent meeting, but in a proper church in New England. And the preacher was not an unlettered itinerant, but one of the greatest theologians America has produced. Hell was a fact of life in Edwards's day for most persons in Christian countries. It was a significant item in their store of beliefs, and was, accordingly, a conviction which gave shape to their lives. Edwards reports that most of the converted in his day were "frequently exercised with scruples and fears concerning their condition. They generally have an awful apprehension of the dreadful nature of a false hope."[3]

By contrast, fear of hell is totally foreign to most modern persons, including Christians. Those who read Edwards's sermon today are more likely to be amused than terrified. It may evoke from them a sort of fear, not unlike the fear inspired by fictional horror stories. Such fear is oddly pleasant, for it poses no real threat since its only basis is fantasy and imagination. Genuine concern about hell seems to be lost in our past, along with powdered wigs and witch trials.

It may not be easy for the modern believer to give proper respect to the doctrine of hell, even if he wants to. As an article published in 1977 put it:

> How can you take it seriously? Hell has become so trivialized that it has even lost its force as a curse. 'Go to hell' is a suggestion friends share. 'The hell it is' is an exclamation of surprise and incredulity. 'Dammit' is something we utter when we stub our toes, not an eternal sentence.[4]

The author goes on to record the following relevant statistics: only one in eight who believe in hell believes it is a threat to him; and among Roman Catholics, only about one third even believe in hell.[5]

While such developments seem more pronounced in recent years, they are not entirely new. Belief in eternal hell was so commonly forsaken in the early decades of the twentieth century that Bertrand Russell was willing to concede in his 1927 lecture "Why I am Not a Christian," that those who claimed the Christian faith did not have to believe the doctrine.[6] As he remarked elsewhere, with at least a bit of sarcasm: "Hell is neither so certain nor as hot as it used to be."[7]

Moreover, this trend away from belief in hell holds not only among laymen, but also among clergy and theologians. As Richard Bauckham summarizes the shift:

> Until the nineteenth century almost all Christian theologians taught the reality of eternal torment in hell. . . . Since 1800 this situation has entirely changed, and no traditional Christian doctrine has been so widely abandoned as that of eternal punishment. . . . Among the less conservative, universal salvation, either as hope or as dogma, is

now so widely accepted that many theologians assume it virtually without argument.[8]

According to a 1981 theology faculty survey—which included questions on a wide variety of moral, social, and religious issues—50 percent of those who teach on faculties of theology reject belief in a place of eternal torment. The doctrine was most widely rejected by liberal Protestant theologians and least widely rejected by Roman Catholics—66 percent of the former and 39 percent of the latter, denied the doctrine.[9]

More recent statistics complicate the picture, however. In a 1990 Gallup poll, 60 percent of Americans professed belief in hell, which is more than affirmed the doctrine four decades earlier. The article which cites these statistics claims "that hell is undergoing something of a revival in American religious thought," even among theologians.[10]

Now it might be thought that the movement away from belief in eternal hell—to whatever degree—and the corresponding move toward universalism is confined to liberal Christians. It may be assumed that belief in eternal damnation is rejected only by those who have given up other traditional doctrines. Surely this is true in many cases. That is, the traditional doctrine of hell is often repudiated as part of a larger theological package which is no longer accepted. However, a number of theologians and philosophers, who are otherwise orthodox, are suggesting and defending alternatives to the traditional view of hell. These persons accept traditional views of revelation and they argue their case on biblical as well as philosophical grounds. Their views can hardly be dismissed by other believers as mere concessions to liberal theology.

Why then have so many theologians abandoned the traditional doctrine of hell? The answer to this is straightforward: the doctrine is widely regarded to be morally indefensible. As such, the doctrine is an integral part of the most serious difficulty posed for traditional theism, namely, the problem of evil.

In his biography of David Hume, Ernest Campbell Mossner tells of an encounter between the famous philosopher and the Reverend John Warden. In the course of their conversation, Warden happened to mention a sermon by Jonathan Edwards entitled "The Usefulness of Sin." At this point, Hume put politeness aside and went on the attack, remarking that Edwards must have accepted

Leibniz's view that all is for the best in this best of all possible worlds. Then, Mossner reports, he burst out, "But what the devil does the fellow make of hell and damnation?"[11]

This incident is a striking illustration of the fact that the doctrine of hell engages us at the emotional level as well as the intellectual. Nothing could be more dreadful than eternal torment, and emotional reactions are altogether appropriate when contemplating the very idea of it. It is an existential issue of the highest order, and if one takes it seriously at all he cannot rationally be indifferent toward it.

This incident is also an illustration of how the doctrine of hell compounds the problem of evil. Indeed, hell is arguably the most severe aspect of the problem. J. E. Barnhart, a philosopher who is a skeptic with respect to Christianity, flatly remarks concerning evil: "If it is a problem, it is the problem of those in hell."[12] And in the same vein, the Roman Catholic philosopher Alfred Freddoso has written:

> there is ample reason for thinking that ultimately the most troublesome form which the problem of evil can take for the orthodox Christian is just this: How is the existence of a benevolent and almighty God to be reconciled with even the possibility of someone's going to hell (whether this is thought to involve simple annihilation or the pain of everlasting separation from God)?[13]

The fact that philosophers who otherwise disagree so sharply can agree on this point indicates that the doctrine is indeed deeply problematic for the Christian faith.

It is not only the case that many who accept Christian faith struggle with the doctrine of hell, but also that many who reject the faith do so because they find that doctrine repugnant. Indeed, popular author Robert Short makes the rather extreme charge that the massive departure from belief in Christ can be largely traced to the doctrine of hell.

> It is almost impossible for anyone to conceive of the trouble this idea has wreaked on the world. . . . At the root of Christendom's turning away from Christ lies the teaching of "eternal torment." Therefore, "hell" is not only the cause of most of the world's unbelief, but also the cause of most of the widespread and deep miseries that unbelief and false belief leave in their wake.[14]

Among those who have rejected Christianity on moral grounds involving the doctrine of hell, one of the better known is James Mill, the father of John Stuart Mill. In his *Autobiography*, Mill reports that his father believed that

> all ages and nations have represented their gods as wicked, in a constantly increasing progression . . . till they reached the most perfect conception of wickedness which the human mind can devise, and have called this God, and prostrated themselves before it.[15]

This perfect conception of wickedness, he believed, was embodied in the creed of Christianity since it taught that God created the human race knowing that the vast majority would eventually be consigned to hell. The same sentiments were expressed by Mill himself in his essay on "Utility of Religion."

> Is there any moral enormity which might not be justified by imitation of such a Deity? And is it possible to adore such a one without a frightful distortion of the standard of right and wrong? Any other of the outrages to the most ordinary justice and humanity involved in the common christian conception of the moral character of God, sinks into insignificance beside this dreadful idealization of wickedness.[16]

For Mill, then, the other moral problems of Christianity are insignificant compared to the outrage of hell.

Similar thoughts were echoed a century later by Bertrand Russell: "There is one very serious defect to my mind in Christ's moral character, and that is that He believed in hell. I do not myself feel that any person who is profoundly humane can believe in everlasting punishment."[17]

Obviously then, the traditional doctrine of hell puts a particularly sharp edge on the already prickly problem of evil. Perhaps it is not surprising that so many theologians have simply dropped the doctrine. Sometimes this has been done explicitly and aggressively. More often, however, it seems the notion has been abandoned quietly and without much fuss. We have gotten along well without it, and few seem anxious to bring up past grievances. The problem of evil is bad enough without the complication of hell, and it seems best to let it lie.

II

Some have insisted, however, that the doctrine of hell cannot be so easily eliminated. Peter Geach, for instance, has argued that

> We cannot be Christians, followers of Christ, we cannot even know what it is to be a Christian unless the Gospels give at least an approximately correct account of Christ's teaching. And if the Gospel account is even approximately correct, then it is perfectly clear that according to that teaching many men are irretrievably lost. . . . It is less clear, I admit, that the fate of the lost according to that teaching is to be endless misery rather than ultimate destruction. But universalism is not a live option for a Christian.[18]

Geach's argument, essentially, is that there is an insurmountable epistemological problem for those who want to be Christians, but deny that many persons are irretrievably lost.

This argument represents, I think, the ultimate reason why many Christians are unwilling to give up the doctrine of hell; they feel they cannot do so while remaining Christians. They believe the doctrine is inextricably connected to the very foundations of their faith. It is on an epistemic par with the very beliefs which make it possible for one to be a Christian. Consequently, one cannot deny the doctrine without unsettling the foundations of his belief.

There is another reason, besides the epistemological one, why the doctrine of hell cannot be easily excised from the body of Christian beliefs. To remove the doctrine of hell may give Christianity a distinctly new shape. It may significantly alter the character of what it means to believe the Christian faith.

At first glance, this may seem like an exaggeration. After all, the doctrine of hell certainly is not central to the faith in the way the Incarnation and Trinity are. It is not explicitly affirmed in either the Apostles' or the Nicene Creed. It appears to be a peripheral matter which is isolated from the main body of Christian teaching and could be lopped off without changing much of anything.

A little reflection reveals, however, that the doctrine of hell is closer to the heart of traditional Christian belief than we may initially think. This is most evident when we recall that Christianity is primarily a scheme of salvation. Its main thrust is a message of how we can be saved from our sins and receive eternal life. Salvation, however, is not inevitable. One may choose to remain in sin and resist God's offer of salvation. Here is where hell comes in: it is the alternative to salvation.

The reality of this alternative has traditionally lent a sense of urgency and moral seriousness to the quest for salvation. It has also highlighted the majesty and glory of God's work to save his fallen children. This traditional picture of what is at stake makes clear that Christianity is not commonplace or trivial.

But if hell is not perceived to be a serious threat, it is hard to see how salvation can have the same meaning it used to. Not surprisingly, salvation is less and less conceived as a matter of eternal life, and more and more as a matter of personal fulfillment in this life. Thus, salvation comes to sound increasingly like a means of dealing with psychological problems, gaining in positive self-image, developing a better outlook on life, liberation from oppression, and so on. I think this represents quite a change in what it means to experience salvation.

If Christianity is indeed primarily about salvation, and if salvation comes to mean something very different when hell drops out of sight, then the doctrine of hell is an important part of Christianity. Indeed, it may be essential, at least in some form, if Christianity is to avoid trivialization.

The fact that hell cannot be easily extricated from other theistic beliefs can also be illustrated by considering the generic belief in God which has been prevalent in American culture. It is this generic belief in God which is appealed to by those who wish to return prayer to public schools. This can be done, it is argued, without endorsing any particular religion. It is important to do so in order to restore the moral values we have lost, for it was belief in God which undergirded the moral values which gave cohesion to American society. Those moral values have eroded as faith in God has declined and so both must be renewed in order to preserve our society. This, at least, is the common claim.

It is not so simple, however, to restore a generic belief in God which is morally relevant. So argues historian Martin E. Marty in an article tellingly entitled "Hell Disappeared. No One Noticed. A Civic Argument." Marty shows that the belief that God punishes evil behavior both here and hereafter is a key ingredient in what he calls "the deistic-theistic synthesis in public education and civic life."[19] That is to say, the doctrine of hell in one form or another was essential to the moral pedagogy of not only the orthodox

Puritans but also the deistic founding fathers. Consequently, a case can be made that those who urge that God must be returned to our schools to undergird morality must also revive the doctrine of hell if the belief in God is to serve as a moral warrant in the same way as it has in the past. This is not practical however, Marty maintains, for the doctrine of hell is culturally unavailable for us.

> I am contending that, if God is restored substantively to the schools and if there is to be anything said beyond the syllable, the concept must have to do with rewards and punishments, now and/or hereafter, apart from soteriological or evangelical proclamation and nurture. Yet if there were to be such a restoration, we would be asking the public schools to make available what is not available in the culture at large, something that has either atrophied or entirely disappeared in the vocabulary and doctrinal repository of most churches.[20]

If this is correct, the fading out of hell is highly relevant due to the fact that the doctrine lends substance or moral import to other vital religious concepts.

Marty goes on to cite the opinion of his colleague Arthur Mann who has suggested "that the disappearance of hell from the Catholic imagination may be the most neglected and most important event after Vatican II."[21] This is a rather strong statement, and if it is so, it must be the case that hell is a matter of more than peripheral significance in Catholic thought. It is, moreover, another indication that hell cannot be extinguished without substantially altering the beliefs with which it is connected.

III

Apparently then, the doctrine of hell is rather tenacious and cannot be easily and cleanly extracted from the body of religious beliefs which have traditionally given it life. And if the doctrine is as problematic as its critics have maintained, this creates some serious dilemmas, particularly for adherents of the Christian faith.

The dilemma is perhaps sharpest for the Christian if both Geach, on the one hand, and Mill and Russell, on the other hand, are correct in their claims. Putting the problem most baldly, if both are correct, a Christian cannot avoid being committed to a moral absurdity. For Geach's argument is that one cannot deny the doctrine of hell without giving up his right to claim to know the very things which make it possible for one to be a Christian. And if Mill and Russell are correct that it is a moral defect to believe in hell, then one cannot be a Christian without being morally defective.[22]

A problem also seems to be generated, though it is not as severe, if both Geach and Marty are right. In this case, Christians must believe something which is culturally unavailable. A belief is culturally unavailable, I take it, if it is not commonly assumed, understood, discussed, and so on, and furthermore is such that what is assumed in the culture at large makes it difficult, if not impossible, to take the belief seriously.

This is a genuine difficulty, but I think it is easily exaggerated. It seems an overstatement to say a concept is unavailable simply because it has passed out of common discourse or lost its grip on the public imagination. Such concepts may be revived, refurbished, and reintroduced into public discourse. What is culturally available in Marty's sense is no doubt constantly changing, due to ever fluctuating social trends. Indeed, as we noted above, the doctrine of hell seems to be making something of a comeback as we enter the last decade of the twentieth century.[23] Moreover, the idea of cultural availability is itself rather vague and elastic so it can hardly serve as a decisive difficulty for the concept of hell.

The other dilemma I mentioned cannot be so easily disposed of, however. It reiterates for us Hume's impatient question: what the devil is to be made of hell and damnation?

While hell has been largely ignored in recent times, there have been some recent efforts to come to terms with it. Two basic strategies have been followed. The first is to argue that the doctrine of hell is not in fact morally objectionable as its critics have maintained. The second strategy agrees with the critics that hell is a morally repugnant doctrine, but argues that Christians are not in fact required to believe in it. To execute this strategy, it must be shown either that Christians are not obliged to accept everything that Christ and the authors of the New Testament clearly taught, or else that Christ and the authors of the New Testament did not clearly teach the doctrine of hell, at least not as traditionally understood. It is hard to see how the former could be considered a Christian option. And the latter, of course, would require that the words of Christ, as well as several other apparently clear New

Testament passages, be plausibly interpreted in ways which do not support the traditional doctrine of hell.

There is a whole spectrum of views on the doctrine of hell which represent one or the other of these two strategies or some combination of the two. There is, in other words, no single doctrine of hell. Up to this point, for the sake of simplicity, I have spoken rather loosely of "the doctrine of hell" or "the traditional doctrine of hell," but now we need to be more precise. So let us consider something of the range of positions on the doctrine of hell, beginning with the traditional view. What follows, of course, is nothing more than a sketch of the various views. My concern now is primarily to highlight the diversity of opinions and the fact that there is no consensus in sight. This information will also provide a useful backdrop for the argument I shall develop in the following pages.

The complication begins as soon as we attempt to state the traditional view with any degree of precision. This can be clearly seen by a look at the well-known debate over hell between F. W. Farrar and E. B. Pusey, which occurred in the nineteenth century. The controversy was precipitated by Farrar's attack on what he took to be the prevailing conception of hell. He made it clear that he did not intend to deny the doctrine, but only certain ways of understanding it. The essence of the true view of hell, he believed, is

> That there is terrible retribution upon impenitent sin both here and hereafter; that without holiness no man can see the Lord; that sin cannot be forgiven till it is forsaken and repented of; that the doom which falls on sin is both merciful and just.[24]

Farrar's complaint was against what he called accretions to the true doctrine which are supported by neither scripture nor the dogmatic sanction of the church. He distinguished four such accretions: (1) The notion that hell involves physical torments or material agonies; (2) the assumption that the punishment of hell is necessarily eternal for all who incur it; (3) the opinion that the great majority of people will be doomed to hell; and (4) the notion that the sentence of eternal damnation is passed irreversibly at the instant of death on all who die in sin.[25]

Although Farrar insisted that he could not endorse dogmatic universalism or conditional immortality—the view that those who do not receive salvation are annihilated—his book was widely read as supporting universalism. Because of the influence the book was having, Pusey, who was Regius Professor of Hebrew at Oxford, undertook to rebut it. In a volume of detailed biblical and historical scholarship, he sought to defend the church's doctrine of eternal punishment, and to show that Farrar had misrepresented it.

His response to Farrar's four "accretions" is particularly interesting. With regard to the first, he maintains that the idea of physical punishment is not an integral part of the doctrine of hell. On the matter of the suffering of the damned, he writes: "Holy Scripture warns us of them and of their intensity; it does not define their quality."[26] He also denies that the third is an essential part of the doctrine, and insists that scripture "says nothing about the proportion of the saved or the lost."[27] The fourth point is not denied, but Pusey attempts to remove much of its sting by drawing a distinction between dying in a state of imperfection and unworthiness (i.e., in sin) on the one hand, and dying outside of a state of grace, on the other. He argues that Farrar assumes that all persons who are imperfect at the time of their death, or who have not repented of all their sins, are not in a state of grace and are thus damned. And since it seems obvious that the vast majority are not perfect or have not repented at the time of their death, the vast majority must be damned.

Pusey counters that we cannot tell by empirical observation who is, and who is not, in a state of grace at the time of their death. "What God does for the soul, when the eye is turned up in death and shrouded, the frame stiffened, every limb motionless, every power of expression gone is one of the secrets of the Divine compassion."[28]

Similar considerations apply to the heathen and others who have never heard the gospel. Pusey emphasizes that the merits of Christ reach to every soul, whether or not they knew him in this life.

> God the Holy Ghost visits every soul which God has created, and each soul will be judged as it responded or did not respond to the degree of light which He bestowed on it, not by our maxims, but by the wisdom and love of Almighty God.[29]

The upshot of this is that none will be lost except those who obstinately refuse God's grace. None will be lost whom God can save without destroying the gift of freedom which he has given them.

Pusey readily allows that persons who died in a state of imperfection will require further purification and spiritual development after death. He insists, however, that our time of probation ends at death. Only those who are in a state of grace at the time of death are saved. But this is mitigated, as we have seen, by his claim that God saves all he can, and that we cannot know who is or is not in a state of grace at the time of death. So then, Pusey agrees with Farrar that physical torment is not essential to the doctrine of hell; he also agrees with Farrar in disputing the popular notion that the vast majority of people will be lost; and, while he maintains against Farrar that it is a part of the true doctrine that our fate is sealed at death, he argues that Farrar has distorted this point with his assumption that we know most persons are not in a state of grace at death.

The point of sharpest disagreement, however, concerns the question of whether hell is eternal for all those who are sentenced to it. In Farrar's view, this is an accretion on the true doctrine of hell. Pusey flatly disagrees and he gives a major portion of his book to showing that hell is indeed eternal. Much of the argument here is exegetical in nature. It involves in the first place several passages of scripture which seem to support universalism.[30] Pusey, of course, argued that such passages, when properly interpreted, do not teach universalism.

Another much controverted issue concerns the meaning of the Greek word *aionios*, which has traditionally been translated "eternal" in such key passages as Matthew 25:46, which speaks of both eternal punishment and eternal life. Advocates of universalism have held that the word does not mean eternal, and that it is used to describe the quality of the punishment rather than its duration. In their view, the fires of hell refer to a temporary, purifying punishment. Pusey argued just the opposite.

With this background, let us sketch out a variety of views which have been held about hell. Let us call the view which Farrar attacked *the traditional popular view*. This is the view that hell is God's eternal punishment which falls irreversibly on all who die in a state of sin. The punishment includes corporeal or physical distress and it will be the fate of the great majority of the human race. This understanding of hell has been held not only by many ordinary believers, but also by a number of theologians.

Next, let us call the view defended by Pusey *the traditional orthodox view*. The essence of this view is that hell is God's eternal punishment of all who obstinately refuse his grace to the end of life. We cannot know the proportion of the saved to the lost nor do we know the nature of God's punishment, though it could include physical pain.

A third view which must be distinguished from the previous two is *the traditional Calvinistic view*. What distinguishes this view from the previous two is the belief that God has chosen who will be saved and who will be damned. The accent here is not on human freedom to reject God's grace, but upon God's sovereign right to damn whomever he will.

The fourth view I will call *the modified orthodox view*. On this view, our eternal destiny is not sealed at death; rather, God continues to offer grace after death, so there is no end to the opportunity to receive salvation. Nevertheless, some will forever reject God's grace and experience the corresponding pain of being forever separated from God. This is how hell is depicted by C. S. Lewis in *The Great Divorce*. An interesting question is whether anyone would be saved on this view who would be lost on the traditional orthodox view. The answer is not clear. It may be argued that those who die outside of grace on the traditional view would continue forever to resist that grace. So the change of circumstance after death would not change anyone's response to grace.

The next position on the spectrum is *the hopeful universalist view*. This is the position of those who find support for universalism in scripture and from general theological considerations but do not think universalism can be dogmatically defended. While they hope universalism is true, they also recognize considerations which weigh against it. Besides scriptural evidence against universalism, and the general tradition of the church, there is the factor of free will. As Farrar put it, "it is impossible for us to estimate the hardening effect of obstinate persistence in evil, and the power of the human will to resist the law and reject the love of God."[31] John Hick conveys the spirit of hopeful universalism by depicting God as a divine therapist who has perfect understanding of each human heart, perfect love for all, and unlimited time to devote to

each patient. While it remains *logically* possible that some will resist God forever, Hick takes it as *practically* certain that all persons
will eventually come to salvation.[32]

The final position I will distinguish is *the convinced universalist view*. Those who hold this view believe that the idea of
eternal punishment is morally unacceptable and, holding to the
absolute teaching authority of Christ, they accordingly deny that
Christ taught it. They interpret the biblical passages in question
much the same way the hopeful universalists do. The difference
is that they are certain that the universalist interpretation must
be correct. Thomas Talbott, for instance, has recently argued that
nonuniversalist versions of Christian theism are implicitly contra-
dictory, and therefore cannot be true. Talbott's view is motivated
not only by moral considerations, but also by the further claim
that the idea of eternal hell finally involves a meaningless notion. In
particular, he rejects as unintelligible the idea that evil can be decisively chosen by free beings. The only account of Christian theism
which is even possibly true, he maintains, is the universalist one.[33]
This is perhaps the strongest form the convinced universalist view
can take.

It should be emphasized that universalists such as Talbott
need not deny that there may be a finite period of existence after
death that involves severe punishment. Such punishment, however, is on their view motivated by love, is of limited duration,
and its goal is the purification and redemption of those who receive it.

IV

The spectrum of views which I have sketched is by no means
exhaustive. There are other conceptions of hell and other varia-
tions on the positions I have enumerated. However, the views I
have distinguished represent the main options which have been
defended by Christian thinkers.

In what follows I will look in more detail at the issues raised
by these various views of hell, especially the traditional ones. My
purpose, broadly speaking, is to show that some recognizably traditional views of hell are compatible with both the divine nature
and human nature. The execution of this task will require some
rather wide-ranging explorations in philosophical theology. Not

only will it be necessary to consider some of the divine attributes and their bearing on the doctrine of hell, but we must also delve into a number of matters concerning human beings which relate to the idea of damnation, such as the nature of human freedom, the process of character formation, and so on.

What I hope to achieve can be stated more specifically in terms of two fundamental problems we have already encountered, namely, the alleged immorality and unintelligibility of the doctrine of eternal hell. My aim is to show that some traditional views of hell can be successfully defended against both of these charges.

It will be helpful at this point to indicate just how the following chapters unfold, relative to these objectives. The first three chapters deal with an array of important preliminary issues, but moral concerns are pervasive throughout. Consequently, these chapters also serve to set the stage for chapter four, the heart of my defense against the claim that the doctrine of eternal hell is immoral. Then I shall turn in the next chapter to argue that the idea of eternal hell is indeed intelligible from the standpoint of human freedom. In the final chapter I will offer some positive suggestions on how hell might be construed, building upon my account in chapter five.

Before moving on to these issues, I want to emphasize that I shall deal with them from the standpoint of philosophical theology rather than systematic theology, even though they arise within the context of specifically Christian teaching. The two fundamental problems I have identified are certainly philosophical in nature, and I shall treat them as such. This is not to say, of course, that a clear line always exists between philosophical theology and systematic theology, and I shall not worry if I cross the line from time to time, particularly since the matters I discuss are of obvious interest for systematic theology.

Likewise, I shall at points engage historical theology and touch upon questions of biblical interpretation, as I have already done in this introduction. Again, this is neither a historical nor an exegetical essay, although I intend the conclusions I defend to be compatible with the results of careful biblical exegesis as well as other standards of historic orthodoxy. But leaving such concerns aside, I hope it will be apparent from the following pages that the concept of hell is a multifaceted one, involving a whole host of significant philosophical and theological issues.

1

HELL AND HUMAN BELIEF

I

The changing pattern of belief in hell is a piece of interesting sociological data as well as a fascinating historical and cultural development. My concern here, however, is with the question of whether the doctrine of hell is intellectually and morally defensible. Even more to the point, is it true? Given these concerns, data concerning what people believe about hell may seem irrelevant. Questions of truth are not determined by public opinion polls or majority vote.

On the other hand, we normally operate on the assumption that there is some correlation between what people believe and what is true. It is, arguably, a basic epistemological principle that if something seems true to normal thoughtful persons, there is at least prima facie reason for thinking it is true. And if something seems false, there is prima facie reason for thinking it false. On this sort of principle, what is actually believed about hell may in the end provide more than just interesting sociological data.

In this chapter, I shall explore this possibility by examining some suggestive arguments which move from observations about the phenomenon of belief/unbelief in hell to claims about the viability of the belief itself. These arguments are particularly relevant to my approach to the problems posed by the doctrine of hell for, as we shall see, they often hinge upon the moral implications of such belief. My aim in examining them is to see if there is some reason to think the phenomenon of belief about hell has any bearing on whether or not the doctrine is true.

17

II

Let us begin by considering an interesting argument against eternal hell, based partly upon the phenomenon of Christian belief on the matter, which was advanced several years ago by Charles S. Duthie. His case is a cumulative one which also involves the testimony of scripture and some emphases in contemporary theology which incline toward universalism. But what is most interesting for our present concern is Duthie's appeal to what he calls "the witness of the Christian heart" or "the feeling of the Christian heart."[1]

Duthie has elicited the witness of the Christian heart by means of a question which he has put to other believers.

> "Granted that the offer of the Gospel confronts man with a momentous choice and that the rejection of this offer may entail precisely this ongoing separation from God, both in this world and in the next, when you look honestly, into your own heart, remembering God's gracious dealing with you and His purpose of good for the whole race—do you or do you not entertain the hope that somehow, in the end, all men, even the worst, will be reconciled with Him?"

Duthie reports that almost all Christians to whom he has put this question admit that they do indeed cherish that hope.

Now Duthie is aware that his appeal to the feeling of the Christian heart will strike some as subjective in the worst sense of the word. What credence should we give our feelings—however deep and sincere—when dealing with a matter of theological truth? Duthie recognizes the limitations of his appeal, but defends it as follows. "Although the last word cannot be with the Christian heart, what the Christian heart feels in this and in other matters must have *some* importance, since it is itself in some measure shaped by the Spirit of God." Indeed, the hope for universal salvation "springs from a spirit so subdued and permeated, despite its sinfulness, by the wonder of the seeking love of God that it finds it intolerable to contemplate the final exclusion of any from the enjoyment of that love."[2]

What Duthie is suggesting, then, is that virtually no Christians really believe in an eternal hell. This is not to deny that many Christians profess to believe that doctrine. But here we may draw a distinction between accepting a claim and believing it.[3] To accept a claim is to be willing to affirm it or assent to it. One may do this even if he does not see the claim to be true. He may, for instance, accept it as true on the authority of another. On the other hand, one actually believes a claim only when it seems true to him. He does not merely accept it as a matter of conscious choice, but rather, he finds himself affirming it because it seems true to him.

There is, Duthie holds, a tension in the Christian heart with respect to the doctrine of hell which is parallel to a tension in scripture between passages which seem to support traditional accounts of hell on the one hand and passages which point to universalism on the other. The tension in the Christian heart may be ascribed to the fact that many Christians think they must *accept* the doctrine of eternal hell, but they do not really *believe* it. In their hearts, it does not really seem true. They find it "intolerable," as Duthie puts it, to contemplate the idea that some will be finally excluded from God's love.

It should be emphasized that Duthie ascribes the Christian hope for universal salvation to the influence of the Holy Spirit. Because the Christian's heart is permeated by God's love he cannot help but hope for all to be saved. Moreover, Duthie believes the movement toward universalism in contemporary theology reflects the movement of God's Spirit. So what we have here appears to be a theological version of the principle that if something seems true or false to us, there is prima facie reason for thinking it is true or false. With respect to the case at hand, since Christians cannot really bring themselves to believe in an eternal hell, despite their efforts to accept the claim that it exists, there is prima facie reason to think the doctrine of eternal hell is false.

How should we evaluate Duthie's argument? There is something undeniably moving in Duthie's appeal to the hope for universal salvation which stirs in many hearts. The wish for a happy ending to the human drama is quite natural, like the preference for a happy ending in a good novel. If the doctrine of eternal hell is true, it spoils the hope for a fully happy ending. Moreover, there seems to be something perverse in not wishing for a happy ending which will embrace all persons. Those who do not share the hope for universal salvation appear to be lacking in love or sensitivity.

However, this is not necessarily the case. We can properly distinguish between regretting the doctrine of eternal hell and hoping it is not true. Both of these emotions, I would suggest, spring from feelings of empathy and compassion. Both are expressions of love and sensitivity. The difference is that the former is compatible with believing conclusively in eternal hell, whereas the latter is not. One cannot coherently believe that something is certainly true while simultaneously hoping it is not. Of course, one can believe something is *possibly* true, or *probably* true, while hoping it is not, but that is another matter. My point is that the feelings of those who hope the doctrine of eternal hell is not true are virtually the same as the feelings of those who conclusively believe the doctrine but wish it were not true. And many Christians, I am inclined to think, are in the latter category. They do not merely accept the doctrine of eternal hell, but truly believe it. They cannot help but believe the doctrine is true, but they heartily wish it were not.[4] If negative emotions or even mixed feelings about the doctrine are not necessarily a clear sign of hope that it is false, the expression of those feelings cannot alone be taken to indicate lack of belief in the doctrine.

Moreover, Duthie's argument is still open to doubt even if feelings of regret over the reality of eternal hell cannot be distinguished from those involved in the hope that no one will be finally lost. The compatibility of hoping for something while believing it is not very likely to happen blocks any direct argument from the existence of a widespread Christian hope that none will be finally lost to the conclusion that Christians "deep down" do not really believe in eternal hell. So Duthie's informal poll will not so easily settle the issue of belief.

It should be noted that our way of construing the feelings of the Christian heart in this connection may have implications for our concept of God, assuming those feelings are inspired by God. If our feeling is taken as one of hope, this may suggest that God does not know whether or not all will be saved, but hopes they will. If God inspires us to hope, and as Descartes held, is not a deceiver, it must mean he does not know of any for whom there is no hope. On the other hand, if God knows all will not be saved, presumably we would not be inspired to hope for universal salvation, for that would raise in us a hope which God knows will not be fulfilled. Another possibility is that God knows all will be saved and is revealing this to us indirectly by inclining us to hope for it. (This is what Duthie seems to be saying). All of these possibilities have implications for our understanding of divine omniscience.

Another problem with Duthie's argument, however, is that it relies mainly on the testimony of contemporary Christians. It is probably the case, from what we know about their theology, that most believers of earlier ages would not have considered universal salvation even a remote possibility, so they would not have been inclined to hope for it. To the contrary, as Richard Bauckham points out, it was the "conviction of many earlier theologians that the blessedness of the redeemed would actually be enhanced by their contemplation of the torments of the damned."[5] Here is another striking example of the gulf between classical and contemporary attitudes toward hell, for most modern Christians would probably find this notion abhorrent and even unworthy of rebuttal. However, we should at least wonder what motivated such a view and suspect that our tendency to dismiss it out of hand indicates that we have overlooked something of importance.

The idea that the contemporary movement toward acceptance of universal salvation is a reflection of God's own Spirit suggests that Christians of former generations were insensitive to God's direction. Or it implies that God revealed himself progressively on this matter because Christians of earlier ages did not have the moral maturity necessary to accept the full message of the gospel. Perhaps the love of God did not "permeate" their hearts to the degree that it does ours, or they were less responsive to it. Otherwise, it seems more than a bit odd that God would wait until recent times to lead the church to such an important truth as universal salvation.

But this is far too favorable to both modern sanctity and modern theological judgment. Modern sanctity does not seem to surpass that of former times, and contemporary theology has departed from traditional views in a whole host of different directions. It would be implausible to suppose that all of these reflect God's own movement.

This is not to deny that important truths, which have been obscured or hidden in earlier theological thought, may become clear at a later time. If universalism is such a truth, it must prove to be more than an intellectual trend in recent and contemporary theology. It must survive careful theological scrutiny; it must be shown to be biblically sound. The witness of the Christian heart cannot alone tell us whether such will prove to be the case.

This point is further established by the fact that the witness of the Christian heart is divided. As Duthie remarks near the end of his article: "Do what we may, we cannot banish from the Christian consciousness the strong words of our Lord about fire, about darkness, about it being better for a man never to have been born."[6] So the witness of the Christian heart does not provide unanimous or consistent support for universal salvation. Rather, there is an inescapable tension at this point.

Duthie's argument does attempt to suggest which direction Christians should take to avoid the dilemma, namely, that they should interpret the words of Christ in such a way that they are not committed to accepting the doctrine of eternal hell. Only if this can be convincingly done will the witness of the Christian heart support universal salvation with clarity and constancy.

Another interesting argument, reminiscent of Duthie's, comes from the pen of Dutch theologian Hendrikus Berkhof. He suggests the possibility that hell is not eternal punishment, but rather, a means of purification, so that all will eventually be saved. He goes on to remark:

> I know that to many this sounds strange and heretical. But the attitude of these 'many' is often strange and cruel; they would immediately warn their nonbelieving neighbor when his house was on fire, but they believe at the same time that he is rejected forever and they seem to be easily reconciled to this fact. Or do they perhaps not really believe it? I think so and I hope so. How could we as a Christian minority live in a de-Christianized world if it were not for the fact that we may believe that God in his mercy knows what to do with all this lack of willingness and power to believe?[7]

Berkhof, like Duthie, starts from the fact that many Christians do not really believe in eternal hell, and moves subsequently to the thought that perhaps hell actually is not eternal. Berkhof, however, does not rely on the explicit testimonies of Christians to establish this fact, but infers it from the attitude and behavior of Christians toward unbelievers.

There is something quite telling about Berkhof's point, for a belief which does not manifest itself in our behavior does not amount to much. Since I profess to believe in hell, I have often wondered what it would take convincingly to *show* this belief in my life. If I am in a supermarket, should I stop all my fellow shoppers and urge them to believe in Christ, lest they be damned? If I am at a concert, should I stand on my seat during intermission and warn everyone within earshot of the wrath to come? While these scenes may strike us as silly, I submit that such actions would be at least plausible for a person who took hell with utter seriousness. For surely, if I knew the concert hall were going to collapse before the concert ended, it would be appropriate for me to warn everyone of the impending danger.

However, such analogies break down. Let us go back to Berkhof's analogy that we would feel it incumbent upon us to warn our neighbor if his house were on fire. How is this different from warning him about hell? In the first place, if his house were on fire, he would certainly want to know about it. And second, he would surely consider it a real danger and would immediately react to it. However, these assumptions do not necessarily hold with respect to hell. It is very likely that our neighbor has already heard about hell and knows as much as he wants to know. He does not consider it a real danger and would not react with anything like the same decisiveness with which he would react if informed that his house was on fire.

Of course, it could be argued that our neighbor must not know enough about hell or he would consider it a real danger, and accordingly react. Although I am inclined to agree with this, I do not think it supports Berkhof's analogy. My point is that the seriousness of damnation and salvation cannot be instilled in a moment in the same way that a person can be alerted to the fact that his house is burning. This suggests that we should persist in trying to convert our neighbor, but it does not mean we are insincere in our beliefs if we decline to warn him of hell in much the same manner as we would warn him if his house were on fire. But perhaps this is all Berkhof meant to imply anyway.

However, there is a deeper problem in Berkhof's argument. He inferred that the attitude of most Christians shows that they do not really believe in an eternal hell, which perhaps indicates that the doctrine is in fact unbelievable. And if it is unbelievable, if it does not seem true to most Christians, it is probably false.

The problem for Berkhof is that this critique has implications which he presumably would not want to embrace. If sound, it cannot be restricted to the doctrine of hell but extends to Christianity as a whole. Consider the following words of Kierkegaard.

> Christianity teaches that . . . every individual, whatever in other respects this individual may be, man, woman, serving maid, minister of state, merchant, barber, student, etc.—this individual exists before God—this individual who would be vain for having once in his life talked with the King . . . this man exists before God, can talk with God any moment he will, sure to be heard by Him; in short, this man is invited to live on the most intimate terms with God! . . . Verily, if there is anything that would make a man lose his understanding, it is surely this![8]

Elsewhere, Kierkegaard observes that men's lives poorly express what they claim to understand, and he remarks that "one involuntarily exclaims at the sight of a disproportion at once so sorrowful and so ludicrous."[9]

Indeed, there is the rub: that such a disproportion exists between the extraordinary teachings of Christianity and the ordinary lives of most people who profess to believe it. What a robust claim it is that we live before God and are able to know him as Father. And what a puny difference this knowledge makes to most believers.

Is it not tempting to think that Christians do not really believe what they profess? If they really believed they could talk to God at any moment, and be heard by him, would they not pray more often, and more earnestly? And if they really believed in the Holy Spirit, wouldn't they live in the Spirit more consistently?

What these questions point up is that being a Christian is *not* a simple matter. The Christian message can be deeply disconcerting and thoroughly taxing if one believes it enough to let it shape his life. Is the demand too severe? Does it make the message itself incredible? If we admit the validity of Berkhof's inference with reference to hell, we might easily conclude that none of the Christian message is true, for hardly anyone really seems to believe it. Thus, the doctrine of hell is probably no worse off than many other Christian doctrines, if we are judging it by the degree of consistency between what believers show with their lives and what they say with their lips.

But it would not do to reject Christianity simply because relatively few of its adherents seem to be appropriately moved by it in the normal course of their daily routines. This also applies to the dogma of hell. Berkhof's mistake does not lie in his indictment of Christians for the complacent manner in which they profess to believe their neighbors are damned. Rather, it lies in taking this complacency as warrant for questioning the doctrine of damnation itself.

Perhaps it takes someone as passionate as Kierkegaard, or as strenuous as John Wesley to make fully credible the claim that traditional Christianity in its entirety can in fact be believed. If we consider that Wesley rode 250,000 miles on horseback, preached 40,000 sermons, sometimes preaching several times in a single day; that the constant occupation of his life was to urge people to believe in Christ and live godly lives; then we are constrained to take him at his word concerning what he believes even if he claims to believe so extreme a proposition as that his neighbors are eternally lost if they do not repent and believe. Berkhof obviously takes little account of Wesley and others like him whose lives give eloquent expression to their claim to believe the Christian premises, including the doctrine of eternal hell.

III

So far our investigation has focused on challenges to the doctrine of eternal hell based on the purported fact that many Christians do not really believe it. Interestingly, a similar sort of challenge has come from the opposite direction. That is, some have observed that many Christians believe the doctrine of eternal hell quite willingly, indeed, too willingly, and have taken *this* as evidence against it. J. E. Barnhart, for example, writes:

> Perhaps a hypothesis worth looking into is that the belief in eternal torment is the expression of the burning rage of those who are frustrated in their ambitions to convert the world to their faith . . . . It is conceivable that the doctrine of hell is a mythologized projection of the worst side of human beings, of human beings in their most vindictive and intolerant depths. Telling us nothing about a supernatural Being, the doctrine of hell perhaps reveals the most imperfect side of the human species.[10]

Barnhart's hypothesis is a specific instance of the more general theory that theology can be reduced to anthropology. In the words of Ludwig Feuerbach, who is famous for advancing this claim, "The fundamental dogmas of Christianity are realized wishes of the heart;—the essence of Christianity is the essence of human feeling."[11]

The feelings of the Christian heart with respect to hell are very different on this view from what Duthie suggested. On this view, the witness of the Christian heart zealously supports the doctrine of eternal hell. That witness, however, is not to be trusted since it arises out of the most wicked feelings of the human heart.

Barnhart is not alone in suspecting that the doctrine of eternal hell is an expression of the worst element of human nature. The same thought is also propounded by the Russian Christian writer Nicolas Berdyaev.

> It is a mistake to imagine that hell as punishment and retribution endured forever in some objective realm of being is the result of Divine judgment. This is an invention of those who consider themselves "good". The human, all too human, idea of hell objectifies wretched human judgment which has nothing in common with God's judgment. . . . God will judge the world, but He will judge the idea of hell too.[12]

Instead of being an accurate depiction of God's moral judgment, the doctrine of hell will be the object of God's judgment. Instead of serving to undergird morality, the doctrine is a perversion of morality by self-righteous persons.

Historical data may also lend a measure of support to this general thesis. In a sketch of the historical roots of the doctrine, Alan Bernstein maintains that the western idea of punishment in an afterlife was first conceived by the Jews as an account of how justice would be visited upon nations which oppressed them. In Christian thought, the idea was further developed in the crucible of persecution. "It was only natural that the survivors [of persecution), like the Hebrews, should try to turn the tables in the only way they could."[13] Thus, the doctrine of hell afforded a means of lashing out at oppressors and persecutors. It was an expression of natural human frustration in the face of mistreatment and of the desire for vindication.

Such a reaction is merely natural, so it does not quite qualify as a revelation of the "most imperfect side of the human species." But on the other hand, such a reaction hardly displays the highest reaches of moral achievement. Either way, the doctrine of eternal hell is traced ultimately to human instincts of dubious moral value.

By this time, many philosophers will be wondering about the point of this whole discussion. For it seems to give too much credence to Feuerbachian theories of belief in eternal hell, and it has been long recognized that such theories usually end up committing the genetic fallacy. That is, they mistakenly infer the falsity of a belief from its questionable origins. In our specific case, it is inferred that the doctrine of eternal hell is false since, allegedly, it has its origin in merely human feelings of intolerance and vindictiveness. But strictly speaking, whether or not such historical accounts of the origin of the doctrine are true is finally irrelevant to the metaphysical issue of whether or not the doctrine itself is true. The most such accounts can tell us is why some persons believe the doctrine of eternal hell. They cannot help us in the more important task of evaluating the doctrine itself.

While I have a good deal of sympathy with this reaction to challenges like those advanced by Barnhart, I think it is much too hasty. As Richard B. Miller has recently argued, such critiques are not always metaphysically neutral. To the contrary, they may have metaphysical implications, and may accordingly be highly relevant to the truth claims of historical religions such as Christianity.[14]

The Christian doctrine of hell is not exempt from historical critique, for it is part of the Christian tradition by virtue of being part of what is presented as a historically given revelation. In particular, the Christian doctrine has been rooted in the teaching of Jesus. Most Christians throughout the centuries have taken it for granted, that Jesus' teaching about hell is morally sound. Any suggestion that this teaching grew out of feelings of intolerance or vindictiveness would be rejected out of hand.

Consequently, it would be very unsettling if it could be shown that the doctrine of eternal hell, even in the case of Jesus, is rooted firmly in objectionable human feelings and instincts. Of course, thoughtful Christians would readily concede that in some instances, belief in eternal hell has such an unsavory pedigree. But the issue here is whether the doctrine was motivated and shaped in the formative period of Christian revelation by merely human feelings of frustration and revenge.

If this were demonstrated to be true, the Christian apologist could not dismiss this finding merely by pointing out that the question of the origin of a belief is logically distinct from the question of its truth. Nor would it be sufficient to mount a philosophical case in favor of hell in order to show that there are other grounds for believing in eternal damnation. Even if such a case could be made, it is not clear that it would lend support to *the Christian doctrine* of hell. Since that doctrine has come to us by way of a chain of historical events, crucially anchored in the teachings of Jesus, it is hard to see how any conception of hell which is cut loose from this anchor could be the *Christian* doctrine of hell.[15]

In principle then, I am willing to admit that the Christian doctrine of eternal hell could be stripped of all credibility if certain facts about its origin were established, but I want to insist that it would be exceedingly difficult to do this in practice. In particular, it is hard to see how it could be demonstrated that Jesus' teaching about hell grew out of feelings such as vindictiveness. The only access we have to Jesus' feelings is through his words and actions. And this evidence would not lead us to think Jesus was vindictive or intolerant. Indeed, he taught just the opposite, urging his disciples to love their enemies and to be willing to forgive them.

Of course, for orthodox Christians, Jesus' teaching could not possibly have been tinged by morally imperfect feelings. If Jesus were God the Son incarnate, he could not have sinned in any way.[16] And if it is sinful to have and to give expression to feelings such as intolerance and vindictiveness, then Jesus could not have done so. But even if it is not assumed that Jesus was God the Son incarnate, it would still be difficult to make the case that his teaching was partially inspired by impure feelings. For Jesus has often been regarded as an exemplar of the highest level of morality, even by those who deny his deity. Unless it is allowed that Jesus' teachings are marred by a glaring inconsistency, it is natural to assume his teaching was not motivated by objectionable emotions.

However, one could sensibly take the line that Jesus' teachings about hell are inconsistent with his other teachings. Bertrand Russell, as we recall, regarded it as a defect in Jesus' character that he believed in hell. Russell acknowledged that some of Jesus' teachings were quite lofty, but insisted that it was a mark of moral imperfection that he believed in eternal punishment.

Russell's claim suggests one way in which it might plausibly be argued that Jesus' teaching about hell was an expression of vindictiveness. If we knew that the doctrine of eternal hell was immoral, and could be clearly seen to be so by any thoughtful person who was morally sensitive, then we could reasonably infer that anyone who believed it was indeed morally defective. And if someone believed the doctrine who otherwise seemed to be morally excellent, we would naturally seek some explanation for this inconsistency. Although other explanations would be possible, one good explanation would be that in this particular case his emotions distorted his otherwise good judgment. Emotions such as vindictiveness and anger would be good candidates to account for the distortion in this sort of case.

What is crucial to this whole line of argument is the certainty that the doctrine of eternal hell is immoral. If this can be shown, the claim that Jesus was morally perfect would have to be surrendered, assuming he taught the doctrine. His teaching authority would be compromised, and indeed, as Peter Geach has argued, we would have reason to reject the Christian revelation. As he has put it, "if the infliction of Hell is very wicked, then there is no reason to believe the revelation telling us there is a Hell."[17]

What is at issue, then, is the morality of the dogma of hell. Those who accept the authority of Jesus and believe he taught the doctrine of eternal hell will deny that the dogma is immoral and will advance arguments to show that it is not, as does Geach. They will rightly ask for counter-arguments from those who insist the doctrine is clearly immoral. The whole dispute will hinge on whether or not a case can be made showing the idea of an eternal hell to be a morally objectionable notion. If it can, then the difficult task of showing in practice that Jesus' teaching on hell was dubiously motivated can perhaps be accomplished. But if it cannot, the charge that the doctrine of hell is grounded in vindictiveness can be dismissed as nothing more than speculation.

But if this is so, doesn't it take us right back to the claim that the truth or falsity of the dogma of hell has nothing to do with its origins and must be settled on other grounds? It does not. Nothing I have said detracts from my earlier concession that the origins of the Christian doctrine of hell are relevant to its credibility. But I have argued that certain hypotheses about the origin of the dogma are plausible only if we know the dogma is immoral. And this, I have maintained, has to be argued on other than historical grounds.

So the conclusion I have reached is in the end similar to the position of those who dismiss Feuerbachian arguments on the ground that they commit the genetic fallacy. It is similar in that it depends crucially on non-historical arguments in assessing the dogma of hell. But it is different in that it grants that certain historical commitments must be made if one is to defend the *Christian* conception of hell. Specifically, one must believe that Jesus' teaching about hell did not grow out of feelings of frustration or vindictiveness.

Before concluding this section, I want briefly to consider a different sort of response to arguments like Barnhart's. This response derives from some of the earlier work of the sociologist Peter Berger in which he argued, in effect, that there are legitimate ways of moving from anthropology to theology. This, of course, turns on its head the Feuerbachian dictum that theology reduces to anthropology.

Berger draws our attention to several pervasive and enduring features of human experience which he believes are "signals of transcendence." He defines signals of transcendence as "phenomena that are to be found within the domain of our 'natural' reality but that appear to point beyond that reality."[18] Thus, instead of construing religious beliefs as projections of the human heart which are illusory, he suggests that certain aspects of our experience reliably direct our attention to a world of supernatural reality.

Interestingly, one of Berger's examples is what he calls the argument from damnation. "This refers to experiences in which our sense of what is humanly permissible is so fundamentally outraged that the only adequate response to the offense as well as to the offender seems to be a curse of supernatural dimensions."[19] The deeds which inspire these experiences not only cry out to heaven, Berger remarks, but also cry out for hell. Such deeds as the massacre of innocent persons not only anticipate hell but also suggest its necessity if our sense of justice is to be vindicated.[20]

If Berger's proposal has validity, if it conveys genuine insight, belief in hell need not always be seen as a perverse projection springing from the dark side of human nature. To the contrary, it may reflect a profound moral sensitivity. But more important, the fact that many persons instinctively find themselves believing that hell is a moral necessity may be taken to indicate that hell is a reality. In this case, the phenomenon of belief in hell would not be used as an argument against it, but as evidence for it.

IV

So what can be concluded from our examination of the phenomenon of belief/unbelief in hell? In the first place, the need for caution is suggested by the fact that this data has been used both to support and to attack the doctrine of hell. Of course, the evidence is not perceived in the same way by both sides in the dispute, but this only serves to highlight the need for caution.

Second, I think our discussion has clarified what it means to have a real belief in hell which is morally credible. It is not enough merely to accept the idea. A person really believes in hell only if the doctrine actually seems true to him and he can sincerely affirm it. Moreover, a credible belief in hell could not be produced only by feelings of dubious repute. Given our fallen nature, much genuine belief in hell may spring partially from dubious feelings, but the point for emphasis is that such belief must also register sound moral judgment.

Whether or not anyone really believes in hell in this sense depends ultimately upon whether or not the doctrine is morally sound. And as we have already seen, there appears little hope of resolving this dispute without careful argument.

The importance of argument for this issue is even more evident when we recall that there is no single doctrine of hell. The question is bound to arise: which account of hell does the data we have been considering either support on the one hand, or undermine, on the other? It may well be the case that certain conceptions of hell are unbelievable because they are morally repugnant, but it does not follow from this that no account of hell can be believed by morally sensitive persons. In the same vein, if we accept Berger's essential argument, we will still want to know *which* concept of hell is being pointed to. Do inhumane deeds, for instance, clearly cry out for eternal hell, or only supernatural punishment of limited duration? Do such deeds demand physical punishment, or would psychological torment suffice to satisfy our outraged sense of justice?

In light of such questions, it is apparent that there is no substitute for detailed argument which recognizes specific differences in the various accounts of hell. What people actually believe about hell is relevant initial evidence, but is it no more than that. We cannot cut short the debate by claiming that no one really believes in hell, nor by insisting with equal validity that some surely do.

2

HELL AND DIVINE KNOWLEDGE

In this chapter, I will begin to focus on the issue of how the concept of hell is related to our understanding of the divine nature. I will begin with perfect knowledge, or omniscience, but I want to emphasize that I make no pretense of considering any single attribute in isolation from the others. It should be apparent, however, that certain questions can best be pursued if we concentrate on each attribute individually.

I

The relevance of God's goodness to the doctrine of eternal hell is straightforward and obvious, but the relevance of omniscience may be less apparent. Strictly speaking, we are primarily concerned with only one aspect of omniscience, divine foreknowledge, since the idea of God's foreknowledge has been thought to intensify the moral problem of hell. To see this, let us recall John Stuart Mill's account of his father's opinion that the Christian conception of God represented "the most perfect conception of wickedness which the human mind can devise." Mill went on to specify: "Think (he used to say) of a being who would make a Hell—who would create the human race with the infallible foreknowledge, and therefore with the intention, that the great majority of them were to be consigned to horrible and everlasting torment."[1]

The notion that God created our world with full awareness that many persons in it would be eternally damned seems to make him directly responsible for a terrible evil. Mill draws this implication when he claims that since God created with foreknowledge that many would be damned, it was therefore God's intention that many be damned. And such an intention hardly seems compatible with perfect goodness.

The connection between foreknowledge and intention is not, however, as simple as Mill's remark would have it. This can be seen by considering the well-known principle of double effect. The basic idea of this principle is that if an agent performs some action for the sake of a sufficiently important good, and if bad secondary effects are unavoidably entailed by the action, the agent is not blameworthy for those effects if he does not intend them. In view of this principle, it is possible that an unintended but unavoidable effect of God's creating the human race was that some would be damned. If God created the human race for the sake of a sufficiently important good, he is not to be blamed for this effect, even if it was foreseen.[2]

Whatever the merits of this argument, the point to emphasize now is that Mill's critique gains its force largely from the particular conception of foreknowledge he assumes, namely, the conception that God has "infallible" foreknowledge of all events, including human choices. This is the traditional view of foreknowledge and it would surely have been predominant when Mill wrote.

In recent times, however, the assumption that God has absolute foreknowledge has been extensively challenged. In particular, it has been questioned whether God has foreknowledge of future free choices. The claim that God has such foreknowledge has been challenged in two different ways. In the first place, doubts have been raised as to whether there is an intelligible ground of such knowledge. In other words, it is entirely unclear *how* God could know future free choices. And second, there has been a vigorous renewal of the age-old debate over whether absolute foreknowledge is compatible with libertarian freedom, the sort of freedom we have if our actions are undetermined, and it is "up to us" what choices to make.

Given such a climate, Mill's remark certainly loses some of its bite. However, the fundamental point remains that one's views on foreknowledge will have implications for his view of hell. This is as true for those who deny absolute foreknowledge as it is for those who insist upon it. In the pages which follow I will substantiate this claim. My purpose at this point is not to join the foreknowledge controversy, although this discussion may have indirect relevance to that debate. My present aim is simply to outline the main options in the foreknowledge debate and to suggest how the concept of hell varies according to the view of foreknowledge one assumes, and vice versa.

II

Views which affirm that God has infallible foreknowledge of all future events have the weight of tradition on their side as well as the apparent support of scripture. Many of those who deny absolute foreknowledge would, of course, dispute the claim that scripture teaches such a notion, although most traditional interpreters insist that it clearly does.

The first view I want to consider is that of traditional Calvinism which commends itself because of its simplicity. It puts forward a winsomely clear account of how God can have fully certain knowledge of future events: in essence, God knows the future because he has entirely predetermined it. God's knowledge of future human choices thus has a ready explanation: they, too, have been determined by God.

Although my exposition of Calvinism is based on the *Westminster Confession*, a classic Protestant confession of faith, I want to emphasize that I am using the term "Calvinism" generically. The view is primarily associated with John Calvin but has also been held by a number of other theologians, both Roman Catholic and Protestant.

Let us consider some of the passages in the *Westminster Confession* which convey this view. The first is a clear statement of the claim that God's knowledge is without limit. "In [God's] sight all things are open and manifest; his knowledge is infinite, infallible, and independent upon the creature, so as nothing is to him contingent or uncertain."[3] The claim in this passage that God's knowledge does not depend in any way upon creatures is particularly important when applied to God's knowledge of our future choices.

In order to see this let us consider the *Westminster Confession's* account of how God knows who will be saved and who will be damned.

> Although God knows whatever may or can come to pass upon all
> supposed conditions, yet hath he not decreed anything because he

foresaw it as future, or as that which would come to pass upon such and such conditions.

By the decree of God, for the manifestation of his glory, some men and angels are predestined unto everlasting life, and others foreordained to everlasting death . . . .

Those of mankind that are predestined unto life, God, before the foundation of the world was laid, . . . hath chosen . . . without any foresight of faith or good works, or perseverance in either of them, or any other thing in the creature, as conditions, or causes moving him thereunto; and all to the praise of his glorious grace.[4]

As this passage makes clear, God is entirely independent of all other persons in his knowledge of who will be saved and who damned because the fate of all persons was foreordained before the world was created. Moreover, God does not predestine on the basis of foreknowledge; rather, foreknowledge is based on predestination.

Another way of putting this point is to say that God is altogether active in his knowledge. He is never passive. He does not, so to speak, look to see who will have faith, and thereby know who will be saved. To the contrary, God determines who will have faith, and therely knows who will be saved. So God is altogether active in his knowledge of future events because God, and God alone, decides what will happen. He knows what will happen by virture of knowing himself, his intentions, his will, and so on.

This conception of foreknowledge is quite successful in making intelligible how God can know the future, including human choices. However, it is far from successful as an account which can preserve human freedom. If God knows future human choices by virture of having determined them, it seems clear that those choices are not free, at least in the libertarian sense. If a person has been determined by God to make certain choices, then presumably he cannot do otherwise than make those choices.

The consequences for the doctrine of hell are apparent. If God foreknew that some persons would be damned precisely because they were predestined to such a fate, then Mill's charge that God intended their damnation seems fully justified. Indeed, on this account, God does begin to look like the perfect conception of wickedness rather than the exemplification of perfect goodness.

The Calvinist cannot resist the conclusion that God intends some to be damned by appealing to the law of double effect, for presumably God could have chosen not to damn any persons. And if God could have so chosen, it was not an unavoidable effect of his choice to create our world that some would be damned. Indeed, if one believes that God is perfectly good and also accepts the Calvinistic conception of foreknowledge, it is much more plausible to conclude that all will be saved rather than that many will be damned. I will return to this in the next chapter, but for now I simply want to stress that the moral problem of the doctrine of eternal hell seems to be further exacerbated on Calvinistic premises.[5]

The next theory of foreknowledge I want to consider represents a focused attempt to maintain compatibility between human freedom and God's knowledge of all future events. I am referring to Molinism, named after Luis de Molina, a sixteenth-century Jesuit theologian, who was one of the main figures in a controversy over the relation between divine grace and human free will. Molina developed his theories of foreknowledge, providence, and predestination as an alternative to the Calvinistic views of his Dominican opponents.

The key to Molina's views on these matters lies in his idea of God's "middle knowledge." Molina concisely characterizes God's middle knowledge as that knowledge

> by which, in virtue of the most profound and inscrutable comprehension of each faculty of free choice, He saw in His own essence what each such faculty would do with its innate freedom were it to be placed in this or in that or, indeed, in infinitely many orders of things—even though it would really be able, if it so willed, to do the opposite.[6]

By way of analysis, let us single out the crucial aspects of this definition. First of all, middle knowledge is so called because it is "between" God's natural knowledge and his free knowledge. God's natural knowledge is of metaphysically necessary truths and is known by him prior to his decision to create. God's free knowledge is of metaphysically contingent truths which are known by him consequent upon his decision to create. That is, it is God's knowledge of which contingent states of affairs will actually obtain and which will not. God's free choice is what determines which contingent states of affairs will obtain.

Middle knowledge is between these two in the sense that it shares a characteristic of each. It is like natural knowledge in that it is known by God prior to his decision to create. It is like free knowledge in that it pertains to metaphysically contingent truths. The object of middle knowledge is what created free wills—or, we might say, persons with free will—*would do* in given circumstances or states of affairs.[7] Propositions which state what free persons would do are commonly called "counterfactuals of freedom."

The range of middle knowledge is infinite. Indeed, it is staggering even to begin to try to realize what such knowledge involves. It involves knowledge of what all creatable persons would do in all possible states of affairs and of all eventualities resulting from all possible free choices. This means God knows an infinite number of things which *would have* happened if the appropriate circumstances were actualized but which will in fact never happen. For instance, consider Jones who dies at an early age. God knows what Jones would have done if he had lived longer and faced such and such situations, whether he would have married, had children, what his children would have done, and so on.[8]

It is important to stress that this knowledge is of choices which are free in a very strong sense. The free persons are such that they could make very different choices from the ones God knows they would make. This means that God has no control over what he knows through middle knowledge. He is passive rather than active with respect to this kind of knowledge. What God knows depends on what choices free persons would make of their own accord.

Molina's concept of middle knowledge can now be related to his views of providence and predestination. The essence of Molina's view of providence is that God arranges the world as he will, in light of what he knows by middle knowledge. God's providence covers free choices in the sense that he brings it about that free wills are placed in such and such circumstances knowing they will make such and such free choices. God's concurrence, of course, underlies all aspects of providence, including free choice. All good actions are specifically *intended* by God while evil actions are *permitted* by God's providence for the sake of some greater good.[9]

Predestination should be understood as one aspect of God's overall providence. That is to say, God predestines specific persons to salvation and damnation only in the sense that he brings about or permits the circumstances in which he knows those persons will freely choose either salvation or damnation.

It is important to recognize that Molina had a number of connected motives for developing his view of middle knowledge. In the first place, he was concerned to maintain that God's knowledge of the future is both detailed and absolutely certain. No less than Calvin, he would insist that God has infallible knowledge of all future events. In a similar way, he wanted to insist that God exercises particular, not merely a general, providence over all of creation. To think otherwise would detract from God's glory. Molina is also interested to defend middle knowledge for the simple reason that he thinks it is clearly implied in certain passages of scripture, including words of Christ.[10] But there is another fundamental motivation at work, namely, Molina's desire to preserve libertarian freedom. This is necessary in order to make sense of the notion that God justly rewards or punishes us for our actions. Without libertarian freedom, it is difficult, if not impossible, to make sense of the claim that some are damned even though God wishes to save all people. For if human beings are not free in the libertarian sense, it would seem to follow that if God wishes to save all, then all in fact will be saved. For if freedom is compatible with determinism, then God could save everyone and do it in such a way that everyone would freely choose salvation.

In Molina's view, it is not possible to maintain both human freedom and a strong view of foreknowledge and providence without embracing middle knowledge. If we want to hold an adequate view of divine foreknowledge and providence, we have a choice: we must either accept middle knowledge or a conception of absolute predestination which totally destroys human freedom. For Molina the choice is obvious. If we accept middle knowledge we can maintain that God's knowledge of the future is absolutely certain *and* that our choices are altogether free—just as if there were no foreknowledge.

Molina puts it like this:

> Thus, while the full force of created free choice is preserved and while the contingency of things remains altogether intact in the same way as if there were no foreknowledge in God, God knows future contingents with absolute certainty—not, to be sure, with a certainty that stems from the object, which is in itself contingent and really able to turn out otherwise, but rather with a certainty that flows from the depth and from the infinite and unlimited perfection of the knower, who *in Himself* knows with certainty an object that *in its own right* is uncertain and deceptive.[11]

It is noteworthy that Molinism has received renewed attention in contemporary philosophy, largely through Alvin Plantinga's free will defense. In most of his formulations of this argument, Plantinga has assumed that some counterfactuals of human freedom are true and that God knows the truth value of these counterfactuals even though God has no control over them. In short, Plantinga has assumed that God has middle knowledge.[12]

Does middle knowledge provide us a way to understand foreknowledge which avoids the severe moral problem posed by Calvinism? At first glance, it seems it may. In the Molinist scheme God does not intend everything he foreknows as in the Calvinist view; some things are permitted only as consequences of giving us free will.

So God can foreknow that some will be damned without intending their damnation. He could still will such persons to be saved and in fact give them sufficient grace such that they could be saved, all the while knowing they will resist this grace and be damned. Recall that God does not have control over what he knows by way of middle knowledge. If God knows such persons would not receive his grace, this is not due to God's choice. Rather, it is their free choice which God knows and it is not up to him how they would freely choose.

At this point, a critic is likely to remind us that foreknowledge, according to Molina, is not simply the product of God's middle knowledge, but also of his free knowledge. So God's knowledge that Mary will make a certain choice in a certain circumstance is an item of foreknowledge only because God chooses to create Mary in that circumstance. Thus, God's foreknowledge that Mary will resist grace and be damned is due to the fact that God has chosen to create Mary in circumstances in which he knows she will resist grace. Consequently, questions about God's goodness remain. For instance, why would God create Mary in circumstances in which he knows she would resist grace if God does not intend for her to be damned? As we have already indicated, the connection between foreknowledge and intention cannot simply be assumed. Nevertheless, the question naturally arises whether it would be better to create Mary in a different situation, or maybe not even create her at all?

Generally then, the assumption that God has middle knowledge may in some respects complicate efforts to deal with the problem of evil, including the problem of hell. Molinism does not seem to be as bad off as Calvinism in this regard, but neither does it provide an immediate solution to the problem of evil. One of the intuitive ways of stating that problem is to argue that it seems plausible that God could have created a world with free creatures which is better than our world. And if God is perfectly good, he would have created that world rather than this world. And in the same vein, perhaps God could have created a world with free creatures in which fewer, or perhaps none, are damned.

This whole line of attack assumes that some counterfactuals of freedom are true and that God knows them. To allow this is, as Alvin Plantinga has remarked, "a concession to the atheologian. . . . If no counterfactuals of freedom are true, then God could not have known in detail what would have happened for each of the various courses of creative activity open to him."[13] By assuming middle knowledge, then, Molinism mitigates some of the more pressing moral difficulties germane to Calvinism, but still leaves the way open to challenge God's goodness from other angles.

If Molinism has an edge over Calvinism in that the moral problems it poses are arguably less severe, it is less adequate in providing an intelligible account of *how* God has foreknowledge. Molina's understanding of foreknowledge depends on his claim that God has middle knowledge, the basis of which seems thoroughly obscure. In one of the preceding quotes, for instance, Molina assures us that God knows future contingents "with a certainty that flows from the depth and from the infinite and unlimited perfection of the knower, who *in Himself* knows with certainty an object that *in its own right* is uncertain and deceptive." This does little to relieve our perplexity. Merely to assure us that the knower is infinitely perfect does nothing to make intelligible how he can know future free choices, not to mention the free choices of persons who will never actually exist. Nor do we find much help in his claim that God knows in himself that which is uncertain in itself.

In defining middle knowledge, Molina suggests that God "saw in His own essence what each such faculty [of free choice] would do with its innate freedom." The idea here seems to be that the created order, including free persons, is somehow a reflection of God's essence. Thus, by knowing his own essence, God also knows the created order through and through. This idea seems sensible enough, but it still does not make intelligible how God could know the actual, undetermined future choices of free creatures. It helps us understand how God could know the *sort* of choices creatures could make, and the *range* of choices they are capable of making, but it does not illumine how God could know the *actual* choices which specific persons would make.[14]

Robert Adams, a contemporary critic of middle knowledge, has raised objections of a similar nature. He doubts that any counterfactuals of freedom are true, partly because he does not see who or what causes them to be true. For instance, consider the following counterfactual.

(1) If P were in C, P would freely do S.

It cannot be that God causes this to be true since it pertains to a free choice of P. Moreover, it is hard to see how P could make it true, for as Adams points out, P may never exist.

> God is supposed to rely on His knowledge of counterfactuals of freedom in deciding whether to create the free creatures they are about; and therefore the truth of counterfactuals of freedom should be prior, in the order of explanation, to the existence of those creatures, and should not be caused by their choices.[15]

It is important to keep clear the distinction between Adams's objection to middle knowledge and the questions I was raising above. I questioned the intelligibility of Molina's account of *how* God knows counterfactuals of freedom and propositions about future free choices, *assuming that some of these are true*. Adams does not think God can know counterfactuals of freedom because he doubts whether any of them are true. He does not, however, deny that propositions about future free choices can be true. These may be true, he allows, because they may correspond to what actually will happen.[16]

Adams does suggest a possible basis for the truth of counterfactuals of freedom, at least when those counterfactuals are about actual persons. He makes this suggestion in a discussion of one of Molina's favorite biblical texts, the story of David in the city Keilah, and Saul's plans to besiege the city in order to capture David.[17] When David heard of Saul's plans, he inquired of God whether in fact Saul would besiege the city, and whether the men of Keilah would surrender him to Saul if he did. David received affirmative answers to both questions, and consequently fled from Keilah before Saul arrived or the men of Keilah had a chance to surrender him. Molina took this story to show that God knew propositions like the following to be true.

> (2) If David stayed in Keilah and Saul
>   besieged the city, the men of Keilah
>   would surrender David to Saul.

For Molina, not only is this counterfactual true, but God knows it infallibly by middle knowledge.

Adams, however, proposes that something like (2) might be true simply because it corresponded to the desires, character, and intentions of the men of Keilah. That is to say, perhaps the men of Keilah were cowardly and prone to treachery. But as Adams points out, the desires, character, and so on of the men of Keilah cannot be thought to necessitate their surrendering of David if he stayed in the city. If their action in question is thought to be free, the men must have been able to act out of character or against their desires. This means that the proposition which is actually true is not (2), but the following

> (3) If David stayed in Keilah and Saul
>   besieged the city, the men of Keilah
>   would *probably* surrender David to
>   Saul.

While this attempt to ground the truth of counterfactuals is intelligible, it is not adequate, as Adams notes, to underwrite Molina's account of middle knowledge. For according to Molina's theory "God knows infallibly what definitely would happen, and not just what would probably happen or what free creatures would be likely to do."[18]

Of course, advocates of middle knowledge are not without replies. Richard Otte has responded to Adams by pointing out that it is no more difficult to account for the truth of counterfactuals of freedom than it is to account for the truth of propositions about future free choices. As noted above, Adams allows that the latter may be true by virtue of corresponding to what actually will happen. Otte remarks:

> But this does not appear to be significantly different from saying that counterfactuals of freedom are true because they correspond to what *would* happen, or what *would* be actual in certain situations. We cannot explain what it is for propositions about future free choices to be true without talking about what *will* happen. Similarly, we cannot explain what it is for conditionals of freedom to be true without the concept of what *would* happen. . . . Both are true in virtue of corresponding to some state of affairs that is neither actual nor is necessitated in any way by what is actual.[19]

Otte's argument seems persuasive to me. However, we must be careful here to note that it does not show that counterfactuals of freedom, or, as he terms them, conditionals of freedom, can be true. If sound, his argument shows only that they are no worse off than propositions about future free choices when it comes to providing a basis for their truth. Thus, instead of seeing the argument as a good case for the truth of conditionals of freedom, one might conclude that it shows there is no ground for the truth of propositions about future free choices. Both are on equal ground, but the ground is exceedingly frail if not nonexistent.

Moreover, even if one is convinced that some counterfactuals of freedom are true, one still might doubt whether they can be known, even by God. For instance, if one does not think propositions about future free choices can be known, he will likely also deny that counterfactuals of freedom can be known. Let us turn now to these alternatives.

III

Let us begin with the view that propositions about future free choices, or future contingents, are neither true nor false. According to this view, a statement which correctly describes what will happen in the future as a result of free choice is not true until the event happens. Thus, the following statement is at present neither true nor false.

> (4) A woman will be elected president of the United States by the year 2012.

However, it will become true or false sometime between now and the year 2012. Given this view, God need not know future contingents in order to be omniscient, for to be omniscient requires only that one know all true propositions, and no future contingents are true since they are neither true nor false.

This view, which Anthony Kenny calls "the most extreme form of indeterminism," was perhaps first expressed by Aristotle and was clearly articulated by Peter de Rivo in the fifteenth century.[20] The view has never enjoyed wide popularity but a version of it has been recently espoused by Peter Geach.

> Future-land is a region of fairytale. 'The future' consists of certain actual trends and tendencies in the present that have not yet been fulfilled. What the Moving Finger has once writ cannot be erased. . . . But ahead of where the moving finger has writ there is only blank paper; no X-ray vision can reveal what is going to stand there, any more than some scientific treatment of the paper on my desk can show what words I am going to inscribe on it.[21]

Given that the future does not exist except as present tendencies, Geach naturally rejects out of hand the idea that God knows the future by somehow foreseeing it.

He does not, however, deny that God has unchangeable knowledge of the future. Rather, Geach maintains that "God knows the future by *controlling* it."[22] This, of course, is the central idea of the Calvinistic account of foreknowledge. But Geach does not wish to embrace Calvinism, at least not thoroughly, so he attempts to avoid the predestinarian implications of his view of foreknowledge by picturing God as a grand master of chess playing a game with a novice. The grand master, Geach reasons, would have complete control of the game. He could even announce at the outset on which square he would checkmate his opponent. "No line of play that finite players may think of can force God to improvise: his knowledge of the game already embraces all the possible variant lines of play, theirs does not."[23]

Geach's attempt to explain how God could know the future by controlling it, but without determining it in the Calvinistic sense is ingenious. It does not, however, succeed in showing how God could have infallible foreknowledge of future actions without determining those actions. As Kenny has pointed out, it does not follow from a grand master's seeing every *possible* move a novice may make that he sees the *actual* moves the novice will make.[24] So even if God knows all possible actions we may perform, and all possible courses the history of the world may take, it does not follow that God knows the actual choices which will be made and the actual course history will take.

But whether or not Geach's argument here is successful is not my main concern. I am more interested in his claim that God cannot know the future by foreseeing it since the future does not exist except in present trends and tendencies. Leaving aside his view that God knows the future by controlling it, this claim suggests that statements like *a woman will be elected president of the United States by the year 2012* are in fact true or false. This particular statement is true if present trends and tendencies make it probable that a woman will be elected by 2012, and it is false if they do not.[25]

A curious consequence of this is that a future contingent may be true on this account, but false according to our ordinary way of evaluating statements. Thus, it may be the case, judging by present tendencies, that (4) is true, even if the year 2012 comes and goes without a woman ever having been elected president.[26] Judging by our ordinary standards, however, if it turns out that a woman is not elected president by 2012, we would say that (4) is false.

Another possibility is the view that future contingents cannot, as a matter of logic, be known. This view is distinguished from the one we considered above by the fact that it holds that future contingents have a definite truth value. It is also distinct from Geach's version of that view for it holds that future contingents are, as they appear to be, about future states of affairs, not present trends and tendencies.

This position has been defended recently by Richard Swinburne. Swinburne thinks that anything God foreknows is, in some sense, necessary. Thus, if God foreknows human choices, those choices are necessary rather than free. Indeed, God's own choices cannot be free if God foreknows them. Consequently, Swinburne argues, we must either qualify the claim that God is perfectly free or we must qualify the claim that God knows all true propositions. Without qualification, the two claims are logically incompatible.

Since he is committed to freedom, both human and divine, Swinburne thinks it is preferable to revise the claim that God knows all true propositions. He proposes a "modified" account of omniscience according to which God has knowledge "of everything true which it is logically possible to know."[27] Since it is not logically possible for future free choices to be known, God need not know these.

Swinburne maintains that his modification is a natural one which theists should find acceptable. He supports this claim by pointing out that theists have traditionally understood God's omnipotence in a similar way. That is, the claim that God is omnipotent has traditionally been understood to mean, not that God can do literally anything, but that, roughly speaking, he can do anything which is logically possible. If it does not detract from God's glory to say that the logically impossible cannot be *done*, even by God, it will not detract from his glory to say that what is logically impossible to know cannot be *known*, even by God.

The move to draw a parallel between omnipotence and omniscience is surely legitimate, but whether it will hold up in this case depends upon whether it really is logically impossible for future free actions to be known. And that, of course, is a highly controversial matter. The legitimacy of Swinburne's modification depends finally upon whether or not foreknowledge and freedom are compatible.

Apart from this issue, questions may be raised about the religious and theological adequacy of Swinburne's view. In particular, it may be doubted whether this view can sustain an acceptable account of divine providence. If God does not have infallible foreknowledge of all future events, is he not likely to be surprised by some developments? Does this allow for the possibility that God might lose control of our world and fail to achieve his purposes?

This sort of objection has been addressed by Richard Creel, who has defended a view of God's knowledge which is similar to that of Swinburne.

> . . . God always knows exhaustively what the future can be, and he always knows what it will be insofar as it is completely determined by his will. Moreover, he always knows what his will will be no matter what other free agents finally decide and do. However, insofar as what he wills is alternatives for free creatures to choose between or among, God does not know which of the alternatives will come to pass. What he knows is that each agent must choose within the parameters set by its powers and circumstances.[28]

The suggestion that God might be surprised is ruled out because God "knows exhaustively what the future can be." Or as Creel puts it elsewhere, God has "eternal knowledge of all possibilities."[29] As the Creator, God knows the range of power possessed by all things, including free creatures. God has set the boundaries and knows all possible choices, and combinations of choices, which can be made within the limits he has set.

The notion that God might need to improvise, or change intent, or fail to achieve his purposes is met by the claim that God has eternal knowledge of "what his will will be no matter what other free agents finally decide and do." Since God knows all possibilities, he could never discover anything new which might literally cause him to change his mind. Thus, God's will has been eternally determined with respect to every possible situation which might arise. As Thomas Morris has put it, God's intentions are

> indexed to, or conditional upon, contingencies arising in the created universe. . . . As many biblical scholars have pointed out, and as the prophet Jonah discovered to his chagrin, divine warnings, announcements of God's intentions to punish, often if not always express conditional intentions. Why can't it always and immemorially have been the case that God intends to do A if B arises, or C if D comes about? This would be fully compatible with an informed reading of those passages which seem to portray God as changing his mind in response to human activity as situations develop.[30]

So whatever choices are made, God knows how he will respond to achieve his purposes. And since every possible combination of choices falls within limits set by God, no combination of choices can prevent his will from being done.

On this view, God is like Geach's chess master. The grand master knows all possible moves the novice may make, but the actual moves are up to the novice. The grand master knows he will win the game no matter what the novice does, but he does not know how the game will develop until the novice actually makes his moves. In other words, he knows he will checkmate his opponent in the end, but he cannot know exactly how until the game unfolds.

Let us turn now to consider the implications of these views of divine knowledge for the concept of hell. The most obvious and striking difference between these views and those sketched above is that from this perspective God did not know precisely who would be damned before he created our world. Indeed, perhaps, no one would be damned at all. And this may provide a way to block Mill's inference that God created our world with the intention that many would be damned.

According to the view that the future does not exist except as present trends and tendencies, God could not know anyone would be damned until those persons were created. Moreover, even if God "knew" that some would be damned, it might turn out in the end that those persons would be saved. Some persons might be tending toward damnation, but later come to repent.

Similar implications hold for the view that propositions about future free choices are true or false, but cannot logically be known with certainty. God's knowledge of the present is again highly relevant for the future. As Swinburne has pointed out, since human choices are significantly influenced by circumstances, "this makes it possible for a being who knows all the circumstances to predict human behavior correctly most of the time, but always with the possibility that men may falsify those predictions."[31] So by knowing present circumstances, God could know it is likely that certain persons will be damned, but this still provides no grounds for God to know, before creation, the likelihood of anyone's being damned.

What is needed here is something like Creel's idea that God, as Creator, determines the powers of created beings, and the boundaries within which those powers can be exercised.[32] As the

Creator of human nature, God could know prior to creation not only the sorts of choices humans could make, but also the sorts of choices they would be likely to make. If God created human beings in such a way that they would be able to reject him decisively, God might know how likely it would be that some would do so. God would not know specifically and with infallible certainty who would reject him and be damned but God might know that it would be probable that a certain percentage of persons would be damned. Perhaps the very nature of moral freedom is such that a certain percentage of persons will invariably exercise it to choose evil. Moreover, God might know the circumstances which would be likely to maximize or minimize the number of persons who would decisively choose evil.

This suggestion is reminiscent of Adams's alternative to middle knowledge. His alternative to the idea that God knows with infallible certainty what all possible persons would do in all possible circumstances is that there might be objectively true propositions about what possible persons would *probably* do in different circumstances. And surely God knows the truth value of all objective probability statements. But as Adams remarks, if God does not have the infallible certainty of middle knowledge, God "must take real risks if He makes free creatures."[33] And this risk, as I have suggested, includes the risk that some may choose evil and be damned.

So on this picture, God might know, prior to creation, that propositions of the following form are true.

> (5) If persons are created with such and such a nature, and such and such temptations are commonly encountered, it is probable that *xx* percent of persons will die in a state of sin.

God would also know more specific propositions of such a structure as this:

> (6) If possible person *S* with such and such a genetic make-up and with such and such environmental influences were to live through such and such situations and circumstances, it is *xx* percent probable that he would go right and be saved.

If God's foreknowledge were so limited, it could well be that his choice to create a world with free creatures entailed at least the positive probability that some would be damned.

Are these views more acceptable from a moral standpoint than the view that God foreknew, with infallible certainty, exactly which persons would be damned before the world was even created? Let us reflect on this question by means of an analogy.

Consider the case of a construction project, say a skyscraper, which involves a high amount of risk for some of those involved with it. Suppose that in the past, it has almost invariably been the case that one or more persons lost their lives during the course of the construction of such skyscrapers. If we assume the director of the project is aware of this, then he will have good reason to think it highly probable that the completion of the project will cost some persons their lives. He does not know exactly which persons will die but he knows it is very likely that one or more of the men who work for him will die.

Now let us change the case slightly. Suppose the same sky-scraper is being built, but the director of the project somehow knows with certainty exactly which man will die during the time of construction. Let us call this man Brown, and let us suppose he is the father of three small children. Let us also suppose, for the sake of simplicity, that if the director of the project were to disclose his information or try in any way to prevent Brown's death, the project could not be carried out.

When confronted with these cases, most persons would, I think, find the second more objectionable than the first. Indeed, most persons would be outraged if informed that something like the second case actually happened in our society. They would insist that the project directors have no right to keep such information to themselves and that such projects should cease.

The first case, however, does not seem so objectionable. After all, cases like this are a commonplace in our society. There are many projects which involve high risk for some of the participants but there is little concern to call these projects to a halt. Indeed, we regularly hear of persons losing their lives while working on such projects. We regret this loss of life but we do not find it an absolute outrage.

Now if my assessment of these cases is accurate, it does lend support to the suggestion that those views which hold that God has only general foreknowledge accord better with our moral intuitions here than those views which hold that God has specific foreknowledge of all future events. Just as we find the first case above less disturbing than the second, so it is less disturbing to think God created our world knowing only that some persons would probably be damned than to think he created knowing exactly who would be damned.

But why do we assess the two cases differently? Is there really any more reason to object to the project when the director knows who will be killed than to the project in which the director knows that some will almost surely be killed, but nothing more specific? Are not both cases equally objectionable—or acceptable? Is it not merely an emotional reaction to be more concerned about a specific person, Mr. Brown, than about persons in general who will probably be killed? The unknown persons are just as real as Brown, we just do not know their names.

So perhaps the moral superiority of the view that God has only general foreknowledge is merely illusory. Perhaps closer examination and more objective reflection will reveal that there is no moral advantage in denying that God's foreknowledge is both specific and infallible. In fact, if what is at risk is not merely death, but eternal suffering, a state of infinite disvalue, it can be argued even more forcefully that there is no moral difference between cases of specific foreknowledge and cases of general foreknowledge.

Indeed, it can be argued that there are serious moral problems with the view that God would create a world like ours with only general foreknowledge of how things might work out. A critic, inspired by James Mill, might express this objection as follows. "Just think of a being who would create a world like ours, knowing it held enormous potential for evil and suffering, but without knowing for sure what course it would take. In creating, he would be taking the risk that a great majority of persons would choose evil, and by his rules, consequently suffer everlasting torment."

It might even be argued, again following Mill, that if God created knowing it was probable that some would be damned, then in creating God intended for some to be damned. So it is not at all clear that the general foreknowledge view is better situated than the specific foreknowledge view to block Mill's inference that in creating our world God intended for some to be damned.[34]

Questions about God's perfect goodness remain, then, no matter which view of foreknowledge one embraces. We will explore the requirements for perfect goodness in a later chapter, but for now I simply note that the general foreknowledge view cannot claim to be exempt from moral problems.

IV

The matter of foreknowledge impinges on the concept of hell in at least one other respect. To see this let us return to the debate between Farrar and Pusey, which I discussed in the Introduction. A major issue between them concerned the meaning of the Greek word *aionios*, which has traditionally been translated "eternal." Part of Pusey's case for the traditional translation rested on the fact that the general consensus throughout the history of the church is that the punishment of hell is eternal. Interestingly, his argument in this regard involved an appeal to divine foreknowledge.

The essence of his argument is that Christ, being Divine, must have foreseen the effect which his words would have on his followers. And since his intention could not have been to deceive his followers, if most of them took his words to mean that the punishment of hell is everlasting, that must have been what he intended them to think. Indeed, Pusey maintained that it is inconsistent to affirm the Incarnation while denying that hell is everlasting. He elaborates as follows.

> Our Lord in His Human mind, illumined by the Godhead with which It was united, must have seen how the words, in which He conveyed His revelation would be understood. Had Universalists been right, He, the Divine Teacher, would have used misleading words, which did (God forbid!) mislead the millions upon millions of His disciples who dutifully took them in their obvious meaning.[35]

This line of argument is one for which I have considerable sympathy. If we are to claim divine revelation, we must believe the recipients of the revelation correctly understood at least the central ideas that God intended to reveal. Otherwise, the purported revelation fails.[36]

However, the argument is not decisive with respect to the traditional doctrine of hell. The defender of universalism might properly point out that there is a respectable universalist tradition which goes all the way back to some of the early church fathers. Moreover, there is not the same kind of deliberate consensus on the doctrine of hell as was achieved, say, on the doctrine of the Incarnation in ecumenical councils.[37]

In light of this the advocate of universalism could point out that Christ must have foreseen that some significant theologians would understand his words in a universalist sense. Furthermore, he foresaw that his teaching on hell would not lead the church to rule out universalism in an ecumenical council. So perhaps he intended his Church to arrive eventually at an informal consensus in favor of universalism—which is the present trend—but it was enough in earlier ages for a minority of theologicans to keep the universalist doctrine alive. While I do not find this line of argument as plausible as Pusey's argument, I do think it has enough force at least to raise questions about his conclusion.

However, Pusey's argument is also interesting as an example of an argument which is intended to show that we can be sure that universalism is false. As I noted in the Introduction, different versions of the doctrine of hell vary according to the degree of certainty they claim. And in Pusey's case, the doctrine of fore-knowledge is essential to his attempt to exclude universalism as a viable option.

This points up the fact that one cannot hold with certainty some of the views on hell which I have distinguished unless one holds that God's knowledge of the future is both specific and infal-lible. In particular, I think this is the case with both the modified orthodox view and the convinced universalist view.

According to the modified orthodox view, God's grace is al-ways available to those who reject him, but some will in fact never receive it. If those who hold this view believe, on the basis of rev-elation, that some will never be saved, they must assume God has specific infallible foreknowledge. For otherwise, God could not know some will never receive his grace.

Again, if it is held that universalism is the only position which is compatible with God's goodness, one must assume God has infallible foreknowledge if one believes God acted in accordance with perfect goodness in creating our world. If God did not have infallible foreknowledge, he could not know that all the persons he created would eventually freely receive grace and be saved.

These cases further illustrate my central point that one's views on hell cannot be isolated from one's views on foreknowledge. As our survey of various views has shown, one's account of foreknowledge imposes certain limits on the ways one can consistently conceive of hell, just as one's conception of hell may entail certain claims about divine foreknowledge.

3

HELL AND DIVINE POWER

I

It is essential to classical Christian theism that God is supremely powerful. This has traditionally been expressed in the straightforward claim that God is omnipotent. Of course, this claim has not been construed by most traditional theologians as meaning that God can do literally anything. Rather, it has been qualified in a number of ways. For instance, God's omnipotence does not entail that he can do the logically impossible, change the past, sin, or create a being he could not control. Because of such qualifications and other puzzles generated by the idea of omnipotence, Peter Geach has concluded that the notion cannot be coherently formulated. What is necessary for Christian faith, Geach maintains, is the idea that God is almighty, which expresses the claim that he has power over all things.[1] Others, however, have been reluctant to surrender omnipotence and have offered fresh accounts of the attribute.[2]

Whether God's power is expressed in terms of omnipotence, almightiness, or the more general notion of sovereignty, it plays a key role in an often repeated argument against traditional accounts of hell. The essential argument is that if God is all powerful, he can save anyone he will; if God is perfectly good, he will want to save all persons; therefore, all will be saved.

The argument gains force because there is apparently nothing logically impossible in the idea of God's saving all persons, if salvation is thought of as simply the provision of eternal happiness. Nor is this feat open to the sort of objections which are raised against the suggestion that God could sin or create a being he could not control. So the argument has a good deal of initial plausibility.

One of the primary purposes of this chapter is to examine this argument carefully, with particular attention to the appeal it makes to divine power. Before doing so, however, I want to take a more detailed look at traditional Calvinism because it has a bearing on this argument for universalism. In the last chapter I suggested that the doctrine of hell is morally intolerable on Calvinistic premises. Now it is appropriate to investigate this charge more fully.

Calvinism represents one of the major options in the history of theology, and is arguably *the* classical position in western Christian theology since it was essentially held in common by such figures as Augustine, Aquinas, Luther, Calvin, and Edwards. Moreover, some of the best-known and most influential writings on hell have come from this tradition. This is the view of hell which has often been identified as *the* Christian view and rejected as morally objectionable.[3] But the main reason for bringing Calvinism under closer scrutiny in the present context is because it shares with the argument for universalism just outlined the assumption that, since God is sovereign, he can save anyone he will. Another central aim of this chapter is to demonstrate the similarity between Calvinism and universalism at this point, and to show how both slide into confusion when they try to reconcile their common assumption with human freedom.

II

The critique of Calvinism which I suggested earlier may have given the impression that it is a simple matter to show where Calvinism goes astray. It is, however, rather difficult to establish an effective case against the doctrine because the implications which seem to follow from Calvinistic premises are often denied by adherents of the view.

As an example of this, consider the following line from the *Westminster Confession*: "God from all eternity did by the most wise and holy counsel of his own will freely and unchangeably ordain whatsoever comes to pass: . . . ."[4] As noted above, a central conviction of Calvinism is that God determines all events. He directly controls all things, and this is how he knows the future. Now if we take this claim at face value, it is easy to see the undesirable implications which seem to follow from it. God appears to be directly responsible for all the evil in the world as well as the good. Human freedom and responsibility seem to be eliminated. Nevertheless, the line just quoted goes on immediately to say: "yet so as thereby neither is God the author of sin, nor is violence offered to the will of creatures." Thus, the seeming implications are denied, so that the initial strong statement must not mean what the unwary might take it to mean.

Of course, this may be perfectly legitimate. It is wise to anticipate misconceptions and misinterpretations and to guard against them by spelling out what we do *not* mean by our statements. All of this granted, however, it remains to be seen whether the claims cited above are coherent, and if they are, in what sense.

Let us pursue these questions by examining more specifically the Calvinistic doctrine that "some men and angels are predestined unto everlasting life, and others foreordained to everlasting death."[5] A crucial element of this account of predestination is the doctrine of God's "effectual call," which is set forth in the following lengthy quote.

> All those whom God hath predestined unto life, and those only, he is pleased, in his appointed and accepted time, effectually to *call*, by his Word and Spirit, out of that state of sin and death, in which they are by nature . . . renewing their wills, and by his almighty power determining them to that which is good, and effectually drawing them to Jesus Christ, yet so as they come most freely, being *made willing* by his grace . . . . This effectual call is of God's free and special grace alone, not from anything foreseen in man, who is altogether passive therein, until, being quickened and renewed by the Holy Spirit, he is thereby *enabled* to answer this call, and to embrace the grace offered and conveyed in it . . . . Others, not elected, although they may be *called* by the ministry of the Word, and may have some common operations of the Spirit, yet they never truly come to Christ, and therefore cannot be saved.[6]

By way of analysis, I first want to point out three words or phrases for emphasis, namely, "called," "enabled," and "made willing." These indicate different degrees of influence which God exercises over human beings. The first pertains to everyone, while the last pertains only to the elect. But as we shall see, it is not so clear who the "enabled" are.

Although all persons are called, it is important to stress that only the elect are *effectually* called. Others are called only in the more general sense that the gospel is addressed to all. Moreover, the non-elect may also experience some limited "operations" of the Holy Spirit, but these are not sufficient to enlighten their minds or renew their wills so that they come to Christ. Without such enlightenment and renewal, the non-elect apparently *cannot* answer the call of the gospel, while the elect, because of it, cannot *but* answer. This is the crucial difference between the effectual call and the general call.

The idea that God calls to salvation persons he has predestined for damnation is puzzling if not paradoxical. Such a call seems ambivalent at best, or utterly hollow at worst. Indeed, the notion of such a call prompted John Wesley to charge Calvinism with making Christ out to be an insincere hypocrite: "If then, you say he calls those that cannot come, those whom he knows to be unable to come, those whom he can make able to come but will not, how is it possible to describe greater insincerity?"[7] Particularly noteworthy here is Wesley's remark that according to Calvinism God can make the non-elect able to come, but will not.

This brings us to the second idea I emphasized in the above quote, namely, that of being enabled. This important concept appears elsewhere in the *Confession*. In an earlier section, it is said that when God converts a sinner, he "enables him freely to will and to do that which is spiritually good."[8] And later, the elect are said to be "enabled to believe to the saving of their souls."[9]

There is an important connection between enablement and freedom. The one who is enabled is made free to will and to do the spiritually good. The idea seems to be that divine enablement counteracts in some way the spiritual bondage caused by sin, and gives the one who receives it ability to do good. He is given an ability to choose good which he did not previously have. This is suggested by the fact that the elect person is said to be "passive" until he is enabled to answer the call to salvation. To put it another way, the sinner seems to be determined to sin in his passive condition, but when he receives God's enabling grace, he is no longer determined to sin. Rather, he is free to choose good in a way he was not before.

The sort of freedom depicted here seems to be of the libertarian variety for if the enablement makes those who receive it free in such a way that they are no longer determined, then nothing is entailed as to how they will exercise that ability. It is up to them. At least this is true in the ordinary sense of the term, and there is no indication that it is being used otherwise. For instance, a women may be enabled to do the good without, in fact, doing it. She may choose not to do the good. Similarly, she may be enabled to believe, and yet not believe. It does not follow from her being able to do something that she will do it, nor does it follow that she will not. It only follows that she actually can do it. Which way she will choose is left open.

But this raises a number of questions, the main one being simply this: is libertarian freedom compatible with the Calvinistic account of predestination? Are the elect actually able to refuse the call of the gospel, contrary to what was suggested above? And are the non-elect in some sense truly enabled to answer the call to be saved?

In response to these questions, let us first note that in the passages above only the elect are said to be enabled. This indicates that the rest of humanity never really has a chance to be saved. Before drawing this conclusion, let us look again at the passage describing the non-elect. It says, "they never truly come to Christ, and *therefore* cannot be saved" (my emphasis). Is there not at least a hint in this line that the non-elect are genuinely enabled to believe, but have chosen not to, and *therefore* cannot be saved? If the non-elect are simply not able to believe, it would be more accurate to say "they *cannot* truly come to Christ, and *therefore* cannot be saved."

This hunch is supported by a remarkable passage in Calvin in which he explains the difference between God's general and special call.

There is the general call, by which God invites all equally to himself through the outward preaching of the word—even those to whom he holds it out as a savor of death [cf. 2 Cor. 2:16], and as the occasion for severer condemnation. The other kind of call is special, which he deigns for the most part to give to the believers alone, while by the inward illumination of his Spirit he causes the preached Word to dwell in their hearts. Yet sometimes he also causes those whom he illumines only for a time to partake of it;

then he justly forsakes them on account of their ungratefulness and strikes them with even greater blindness.[10]

Notice what Calvin says here: sometimes God gives even the non-elect genuine illumination, but "only for a time." And why only for a time? Because of their "ungratefulness." This surely suggests that at least some of the non-elect are actually enabled to believe and be saved. It implies that they really could receive God's grace with gratitude, but choose not to, and for that reason God "justly forsakes them." Otherwise, it would hardly make sense to say their rejection of the gospel is a fitting occasion for "severer condemnation."

But again, this raises serious questions. Is it really possible that some of the persons who were predestined by God for damnation before the world was created could actually believe and be saved? Of course, it is possible in the sense that God could have elected those persons for salvation. But since he has not, their salvation is not possible if God's unchangeable decrees are to stand.

Then what is to be made of this passage with its apparent teaching that even some of the non-elect actually could respond to the gospel in a saving way? Charitably interpreted, it represents an attempt to make sense of how God can be willing to save persons he himself has chosen to damn. This notion, like the notion that God calls the non-elect, is paradoxical to say the least. At its best, the passage is also a valiant effort to show how God can be just in damning the non-elect.

But a less charitable reading of the passage lends support to Wesley's charge that Calvinism makes God insincere. It can easily be read in such a way that it seems God is toying with the lost. He gives them a temporary ability to believe, but in the end it must be withdrawn, for they have been chosen for damnation. For according to Calvinism, if God were truly willing to save such persons, their "ungratefulness" would not stand in the way. Indeed, such persons would never have been ungrateful in the first place, or God would simply determine them to cease their ingratitude and accept grace with thankfulness.

This brings us to the third idea I singled out in the quote above, namely, that of being made willing. This notion differs from the idea of being enabled in the important respect that it involves a more determinate action on God's part. If God makes a person willing to do the good, then that person will surely will to do the good. By contrast, a person who is enabled to will to do the good may or may not will it. The person who is enabled can will either way but the one who is made willing is determined to will as he has been made to will. Indeed, it seems he cannot will otherwise.

This is indicated by the following line from Calvin, which points up the difference between being enabled and being made willing: "He [God] does not move the will in such a manner as has been taught and believed for many ages—that it is afterward in our choice either to obey or resist the motion—but by disposing it efficaciously."[11] Although Calvin does not use the words "enable" and "make willing," the concepts are clearly there. His account of the will being moved in such a way that afterward one has the choice to obey or resist is a good description of what it means to be enabled. As opposed to this, Calvin prefers the notion that God disposes the will efficaciously, which corresponds to what we have meant by being made willing. This recalls the concept of God's effectual calling, which can now be seen to be essentially the same as that of being made willing.

These concepts underwrite the claim that God can save anyone he will. He can make a sheep out of any wolf he pleases. If an elect sheep-to-be is at first a particularly obstinate wolf, God effectually subdues him by "a more powerful grace." Furthermore, when the obstinate are not converted, it is because God "does not manifest that more powerful grace, which is not lacking if he should please to offer it."[12]

So it seems to follow from what Calvin says that if God elects to make a person willing to come to Christ, it is not within that person's power to be unwilling to come to Christ. God exercises power in election, and if salvation depends solely on his sovereign and unilateral choice, obviously, no one can resist. But of course if a person has been made willing to come to Christ, he would not want to resist. Indeed, the *Confession* says that those who come to Christ "come most freely, being made willing by his grace."

This brings us to a point of crucial importance. We saw earlier that divine enablement produces freedom, and the freedom involved seems to be of the libertarian variety. Now we see freedom described as the result of being made willing. The point for emphasis is that this latter freedom cannot be libertarian. For, as Thomas Flint has put it, the heart and soul of libertarianism is the conviction that what an agent does freely is genuinely up to the agent to do freely or to refrain from doing freely; no external circumstance, no other agent, does or even can determine what I do freely.[13]

This sort of freedom is clearly ruled out for those who are made willing by God. So the claim that the choices in question are free must somehow be compatible with the claim that God determines those choices. In short, freedom and determinism must be compatible.

This, of course, is a widely held view in contemporary philosophy. Many philosophers believe a sufficient account of free action can be given even if it is held that all actions are strictly determined by factors such as natural laws and/or God. Such actions, it is argued, can still be done willingly and without constraint. Indeed, philosophers who hold this view typically maintain that we are even able to do other than we are determined to do.

This is perhaps the most counterintuitive claim made by compatibilists, for it is hard to see how a person who is determined to perform some action could avoid it. Compatibilists have, however, accepted the challenge to defend this claim. The most common argument in this regard is that statements of ability are actually disguised conditionals. Thus, to say, for instance, that Wesley could have married a different woman than he did is to say something like the following.

> If Wesley had chosen to marry a different woman than he did, then he would have married a different woman, and he could have chosen to marry a different woman.

The obvious question this raises, however, is how, on deterministic premises, Wesley *could have* chosen to marry a different woman. The compatibilist is thus required to analyze the "could have" in his conditional if it is to explain anything. While compatibilists have also accepted this challenge, critics have found their more complicated analyses of statements of ability no more satisfying than their simpler ones. So it remains doubtful whether compatibilists can give any meaningful sense to their claim that a person whose actions are determined is able to do other than he does.[14]

But let us come back to the idea that an action can be caused or determined without being constrained. This conviction, which is at the heart of compatibilism, has often been illustrated by the phenomenon of hypnosis. For instance, Antony Flew, who argues that determinism and freedom are compatible, appeals to hypnosis to support the claim that freedom and the Calvinistic doctrine of predestination are similarly compatible. That is to say, Calvinism "makes out that all of us, all the time, whether we know it or not . . . are, really and ultimately, as it were acting out the irresistible suggestions of the Great Hypnotist."[15] Thus, we are not constrained, because from the standpoint of subjective experience, we have no sense that we are being controlled, even as a hypnotized person thinks he is acting entirely of his own accord.

Now this seems to be the sense in which those who are made willing come to Christ "most freely," for they are not free in the libertarian sense that it is genuinely up to them whether or not they will respond favorably to God's grace and come to Christ. From the standpoint of subjective experience, it might seem that it is up to them whether or not to accept Christ, but if God has in fact made them willing to do so, then it is not. Likewise, the non-elect freely sin and freely reject Christ. Their choices are "free" even though they are determined, because they sin willingly and without constraint.[16]

It might be argued in response to this that just because a person's *will* is determined, it does not follow that his *actions* are determined. A person might act contrary to his own will in the sense that he may choose to do something even though he is not really willing to do it. He may do it very unwillingly. Therefore, a person who was made willing to receive Christ would not necessarily be determined to receive him, and a sinner who was determined not to *will* the good may still choose to *do* it.

But even if this is granted, such choices would not be *free* choices according to the *Westminster Confession*. For it is clearly affirmed that God's sovereignty does no violence to the will of creatures. This surely means that free choices are those which are made in accordance with one's will, not contrary to it. So freedom consists in choosing to do what God has made one willing to do, not in the ability to choose otherwise. If a woman can choose not to do something which God has made her willing to do, and she so chooses, then God does violence to her will by making her willing to do what she herself chooses not to do.[17] Conclusions like this suggest that it may not even be coherent to think one could choose not to do something which God made one willing to do, compatibilism notwithstanding.

III

In view of this analysis, a number of questions must be pressed. First, are the ideas of being enabled and being made willing compatible? As I have already noted, the *Westminster Confession* makes use of both these concepts in describing God's action on behalf of the elect.

It is possible, I think, to construct a model of God's action in which the two are compatible. For instance, one might say God enables an elect person to believe, and if he chooses to, that is all that is necessary to secure his salvation. But if the person chooses not to believe, even after being enabled, then God makes him willing to believe. Either way, he ends up believing and God's election of the person to salvation is accomplished. On this model, some of the elect require only enablement, but others must be made willing, depending on what degree of obstinance they display. So there is no inconsistency in saying that God both enables and makes willing in behalf of his elect.

But this does not entirely resolve the issue, for the real question is whether it is coherent to claim that God simultaneously enables a person to believe while also making him willing to believe. Again, I think a positive answer can be returned. It may be the case that it is not enough for salvation to make a person willing to believe, for he might want to believe but be unable to do so. Thus, God must enable him to believe as well as make him willing to believe. Indeed, if what I argued above is correct, namely, that if God makes a person willing to do something, he cannot do otherwise, then perhaps it is always implicit that if God makes a person willing to do something, he is able to do it.

Although it may be true that the idea of being made willing by God implies enablement or ability of some sort, it is not the case that ability implies anything about willingness. And when enablement is understood in the normal sense, it is incompatible with the idea of being made willing. There are then two distinct conceptions of enablement.

(1) Because P is determined to do A by being made willing to do A, P is able to do A.

(2) P is enabled to do A, but it is up to P whether or not he does A.

The second of these, I think, is the normal understanding of what it means to be enabled to do something, and is also the natural way to read those passages in the *Westminster Confession* in which the idea appears.

When enablement is understood this way, it implies a libertarian view of freedom, as I have already pointed out. Because of this consequence, it is not enough for the Calvinistic view of election for persons merely to be enabled to come to Christ. For if a person is enabled to come to Christ, but not made willing, it is finally up to him whether or not to accept salvation. This, of course, is completely at odds with the Calvinistic view of election, according to which God, and God alone, decides who will be saved. In order to underwrite this strict view of election, it must be maintained that the elect are made willing to come to Christ.

Thus, there is finally an inconsistency in saying both that God enables a person to come to Christ *and* makes him willing to do so. The idea of being enabled must give way to that of being made willing in order to give a consistent sense to Calvinism. And this means there is no room in a Calvinistic framework for libertarian freedom. Although the *Westminster Confession* seems to want it both ways, the only kind of freedom which can be maintained is of the compatibilist variety, that is, freedom which is compatible with determinism.

It might be objected that there is room for libertarian freedom if some of the elect respond favorably to enablement and do not therefore require being made willing. Such persons could plausibly be thought to retain libertarian freedom. The fact remains, however, that such persons could never choose otherwise if they are really the elect. A further problem with this suggestion is that it is doubtful whether Calvinism conceives of God acting in this way. The more likely interpretation is that God makes all of the elect willing to come to Christ.

This brings us to a second question: Is this view of freedom consistent with the claim that God is perfectly good? In the previous chapter, I suggested that if God is perfectly good, it is more natural to conclude from Calvinistic premises that all will be saved rather than that many will be damned. Now that we have looked at Calvinism more carefully, I think this conclusion is fully justified.

For if freedom and determination are compatible, and persons are free only in the sense that they do what God has made them willing to do, then God could save all persons with their freedom intact. Not only could God save all persons, but he could also eliminate all evil and do it in such a way that all would obey his will "most freely." He could, but he will not.

Now if God could save all persons in this manner, but will not, it is hard to see how he could be thought loving, just, or good. Apparently the Westminster divines felt this tension also, as the following paragraph on the non-elect suggests.

> The rest of mankind God was pleased, according to the unsearchable counsel of his own will, whereby he extendeth or withholdeth mercy as he pleaseth, for the glory of his sovereign power over his creatures, to pass by, and to ordain them to dishonour and wrath for their sin, to the praise of his glorious justice.[18]

On the one hand, the appeal to the "unsearchable counsel" of God's will seems to discourage as futile any attempt to understand or justify God's decrees. This implies that we neither are supposed to see the correlation between God's will and his goodness, nor to question it. On the other hand, two grounds are offered for why God elects not to save some people, namely "for the glory of his sovereign power over his creatures," and second, for the "praise of his glorious justice,"

Once again, I think we have a case of wanting to have it both ways, when only one can be consistently held. For if God's power, or the glorification of his power, is in some way supposed to be a sufficient ground for damning some people, then justice is an irrelevant consideration. If for example, merely having the power to do something somehow itself justifies doing it, there is no more to be said.[19] God could then, it seems, show the glory of his sovereign power by creating a world of saints and condemning them all to an eternal hell, even if they never sinned, or a world in which he caused everyone to sin grossly but then change all of them in such a way that they could enjoy the glories of heaven. Either way, God's sovereign power would be equally manifest. Thus, God's electing some for heaven and passing over others is only one of several ways his power could be shown. So it is pointless to ask why God chose to save some, rather than all, or none. To do so is to try to search the unsearchable.

The Westminster divines, however, were not content to leave things there for they went on to claim that election shows God's "glorious justice." This implies that God's power, or the glorification of his power, is not a sufficient explanation for passing over the non-elect, or at least that it is not the only explanation available. It is also the case that damnation is the just punishment for their sin. But this claim can be highly misleading unless we take it in the context of points we have already discussed.

Normally, when we say a punishment is just, we assume the person involved could have refrained from his wrong actions. We also assume a common standard of judgment for all persons, so that none are arbitrarily punished or exempted from punishment. However, neither of these assumptions holds with respect to God's treatment of the non-elect. There seems to be no meaningful sense in which they are able to avoid the sin for which they are condemned.[20] Like the elect, they do only what they are determined to do, but the elect are saved, whereas they are ordained to suffer God's wrath. God, and God alone, simply decides which persons will be left in sin, and which persons will be made willing to receive Christ.

When the claim that election shows God's justice is thus qualified, it does not amount to much. We are still left with God's sovereign power as the sole ground of his electing some for salvation and passing over the rest. Thus, justice collapses into sovereign power, just as the idea of being enabled collapses into the notion of being made willing.

Overall, then, we have discerned two conflicting streams of thought in Calvinism. One stream flows from the idea of all people being called and enabled by God, and suggests libertarian freedom so that punishment for sin is a matter of justice. The other stream flows from the idea of people being made willing by God, which bases damnation on God's power to do with his creatures as he will. Although the former of these is necessary to maintain God's goodness, it is inevitably swallowed up by the latter, which is necessary to sustain the Calvinistic account of election.

The fact that Calvinism has these two conflicting streams of thought is, I think, quite significant. It may explain how Calvinists can, with an air of plausibility, deny the unwelcome implications which follow from their premises. By trading on both conceptions of freedom, it seems possible to hold both that God determines all things in the strictest sense, and that human beings are truly responsible for their sin. This effectively obscures the implication that God could save all people, and in such a way that all would come to Christ "most freely." When libertarian freedom slips into Calvinism, the Calvinist may find himself thinking that God really is willing to save the non-elect, and that they have rejected a genuine opportunity for salvation. In this frame of mind, the Calvinist believes simultaneously that God can save anyone he will *and* that sinners can successfully resist God's grace.

If the preceding argument is correct, such a position is ultimately due to confusion. In saying this, I do not mean to suggest the confusion is deliberate or intentional. Indeed, the Westminster divines probably fell into this confusion in a sincere effort to reconcile Calvinism with some very common basic moral intuitions. They were properly motivated by a desire to give full recognition to God's omnipotence. It seems they did not clearly see that if human beings are free in the libertarian sense, it is no compromise of God's omnipotence to admit he might not be able to save anyone he will. And rather than compromise omnipotence, they concluded that God has chosen to damn some persons, even though he could save them.

IV

Let us turn now to a more careful examination of the argument for universalism I sketched at the beginning of this chapter. John Hick states it as follows.

> For the doctrine of hell has as its implied premise either that God does not desire to save all His human creatures, in which case He is only limitedly good, or that His purpose has finally failed in the case of some . . . of them, in which case He is only limitedly sovereign.

> I therefore believe that the needs of Christian theodicy compel us
> to repudiate the idea of eternal punishment.[21]

Hick's argument, if sound, leaves the traditional theist with no option but to embrace universalism. Taken at face value, his claim is
that it follows by logical necessity from traditional theistic premises
that all will be saved. The only way one can consistently deny universalism is by revising or rejecting the traditional view of God.
That is, one must either revise or reject the claim that God is
perfectly good or that he is fully sovereign.

But is this argument sound? Before we attempt to answer
this, it will be instructive to compare the following, much quoted,
argument of J. L. Mackie with that of Hick. Mackie claims there is
a contradiction between these propositions: God is omnipotent,
God is wholly good; and yet evil exists. He attempts to make the
contradiction explicit by spelling out the 'additional principles'

> that good is opposed to evil, in such a way that a good thing clim-
> inates evil as far as it can, and that there are no limits to what
> an omnipotent thing can do. From these it follows that a good
> omnipotent thing eliminates evil completely, and then the propo-
> sitions that a good omnipotent thing exists, and the evil exists, are
> incompatible.[22]

Since it is obvious that evil exists, Mackie draws the conclusion
that a good, omnipotent being does not exist.

What is striking is the similarity of these two arguments. They
share the same structure and essentially the same premises. That
is, they agree that the existence of evil is incompatible with the
existence of a God who is fully good and omnipotent. There is, of
course, also a significant difference. For Mackie, it is the evil in this
present life which is incompatible with God's existence, while for
Hick it is the everlasting evil of hell which is incompatible with
God's existence.

Now this raises the question of how Hick can believe in God
in the face of evil since he thinks evil cannot, in the end, co-exist
with a fully good omnipotent being. How is it that God and evil
can presently exist together?

In response to this, Hick appeals to the need for a "degree
of genuine freedom and independence" from God if human beings are to enjoy an "authentic personal relationship with Him."[23]

Without such freedom, Hick sees no point in God's creating finite creatures. But while such freedom is necessary for a real relationship with God, it can be abused. Indeed, given such freedom, Hick thinks it virtually inevitable that humanity fell into sin. Moreover, much of the evil and suffering which have characterized human history is due to the abuse of free will. In short then, Hick's position appears to be that the existence of evil is temporarily compatible with the existence of a perfectly good, omnipotent being, but not ultimately so.

At this point, Hick and Mackie part company, for Mackie does not think the free will of creatures should be even a temporary barrier for an omnipotent God:

> If there is no logical impossibility in a man's freely choosing the good on one, or on several, occasions, there cannot be a logical impossibility in his freely choosing the good on every occasion. God was not, then, faced with a choice between making innocent automata and making beings who, in acting freely, would sometimes go wrong: there was open to him the obviously better possibility of making beings who would act freely but always go right. Clearly, his failure to avail himself of this possibility is inconsistent with his being both omnipotent and wholly good.[24]

Now if Mackie is right, there is no room at all for moral evil to co-exist with a good, omnipotent, and omniscient God. And initially, at least, his claim is quite plausible.

However, it is generally agreed that Mackie's argument has been successfully refuted by Alvin Plantinga in his well-known "free will defense." There is no need here for a full summary, but I do want to emphasize the main thrust of his answer to Mackie, for I think it is quite relevant to Hick's argument against eternal hell.

Plantinga grants, in the first place, that it is indeed logically possible that there exist a world containing free creatures who always choose what is right. In fact, there are many such possible worlds, or possible complete states of affairs. But the crucial question for the free will defense is whether it is within God's power to create any possible world he pleases.[25] And while at first sight the answer seems to be yes, perhaps it is no. For if persons are free in the libertarian sense, it is partly up to them which worlds

God can create. Not every world which is possible, in the sense that it represents a logically consistent, complete state of affairs, is one which God can create. Or as Thomas Flint has put it, not all worlds which are possible for God to actualize are feasible for him. In view of this, we can say that "the set of worlds which are possible for God to actualize is identical to the set of all possible worlds, whereas the set of worlds which are feasible for him is necessarily a proper subset thereof."[26]

The fact that free creatures can limit which worlds God can create can be easily seen from the following. Consider a possible world which includes the state of affairs S that all persons are able to go right or wrong with respect to a certain moral action A. No matter how the persons would choose, there is a possible world which God could not create. If all persons would go right with respect to A, then God could not create any world in which S obtains and in which some persons go wrong with respect to A. Likewise, if some would go wrong with respect to A, then God could not create any world in which S obtains and all persons go right with respect to A. This means that the choices of these persons will determine which of the two worlds God can create. Moreover, it is at least possible that all possible persons would go wrong with respect to some moral actions. And if all would in fact do so, God could not create *any* world with free creatures without permitting moral evil. Whether or not God knows which choices would be made by all possible persons depends, of course, on whether or not he has middle knowledge.[27]

The relevance of Plantinga's argument to the doctrine of eternal hell is apparent. For if we are free either to accept or reject God's offer of salvation, then perhaps God, even though omnipotent, *cannot* save everyone. Some may decisively choose to reject salvation, and if they do, God cannot save them without revoking their freedom. Thus, Hick's argument for universalism fails.

Now the remarkable thing is that Hick admits that human freedom is a problem for universalism. As noted above, he believes that much of the evil in this present world is due to the fact that we are free and have misused our freedom. And if we are able to disobey God now, even though he is perfectly good and omnipotent, it seems reasonable to think we could continue to do so forever. Hick seems to concede this.

There would be a logical contradiction in its being, in the strict sense, *predetermined* that creatures endowed with free will shall come to love and obey God. For the thoughts and actions of free beings are in principle unknowable until they occur. They cannot therefore be made the subject of absolute predictions. It would infringe the nature of the personal order if we could assert as a matter of assured knowledge that all men *will* respond to God.[28]

It is interesting to see exactly why Hick thinks human freedom precludes an absolute universalist position. The main reason seems to be that future free actions are unknowable in principle, so it cannot be known with certainty that all persons will accept salvation. Thus, by embracing this view, Hick appears to be embracing the view that God has only general foreknowledge.

The essential idea of free action which Hick affirms is that free action arises out of an agent's character, but "not in a fully determined and predictable way." Free choices are unpredictable because "the character is itself partially formed and partially reformed in the very moment of free decision."[29]

Now this seems to create a dilemma for Hick. On the one hand, his initial argument is that universalism is a certainty. It follows, as a matter of logical necessity, that if God is perfectly good and sovereign, then all will be saved. But on the other hand, Hick affirms a conception of freedom from which it follows that universalism is, at best, contingently true. Moreover, given Hick's view that future contingents are in principle unknowable, it is hard to see how universalism could be an epistemological certainty. If not even God can know future free choices, then no one can know with certainty that all will be saved. And yet, Hick concludes his discussion by insisting that "we may confidently affirm the ultimate salvation of all God's children."[30]

So Hick seems to suggest two incompatible positions, and it is not clear to which of them he is ultimately committed. His indecision, if not confusion, is further displayed in the following.

However long an individual may reject his Maker, salvation will remain an open possibility to which God is ever *trying* to draw him . . . . It seems morally (although still not logically) impossible that the infinite resourcefulness of infinite love working in unlimited time should be eternally *frustrated*, and the creature reject its own good, presented to it in an endless range of ways...despite the logical possibility of *failure* the probability of [God's] success amounts, as it seems to me, to a practical certainty.[31]

Again, Hick admits that the nature of human freedom is such that some persons might resist God's love forever. So it is not necessarily true that if God is perfectly good and omnipotent, then all will be saved. The most Hick can consistently claim is that if God is of such a nature, then very probably all will be saved. If this is what he is saying, than his claim is at least initially plausible. Whether it is ultimately plausible I will not say at this point, but I will come back to this question in the next chapter.

For now I want to point out that in the passage above, Hick seems to smuggle into his argument at least the suggestion that if all are not saved, then God is not fully omnipotent. And this takes us back to his original claim that universalism is entailed if God is both perfectly good and omnipotent. Notice the words I have emphasized in the quote from Hick. He speaks of God as trying to save all people, as being frustrated if he cannot, and even goes so far as to say it would be a failure on God's part if all are not saved. While such language is often fitting for fallible, finite beings, it hardly seems appropriate for an infinite God. As Geach has remarked: "Nobody can deceive God or circumvent him or frustrate him; and there is no question of God trying to do anything and failing."[32]

To say that someone is trying to do something is normally to imply that he does not know the outcome of his efforts. He hopes to succeed, and perhaps he will, but perhaps he will not. To say that he is frustrated is to suggest he has encountered difficulties he never expected and does not know how to deal with them. To say that someone has failed is to imply he thought he could do something, but found out otherwise when he tried it.

Now it might be objected that such language is appropriate, given Hick's view that God has only a general foreknowledge of future free choices. For if God does not have infallible foreknowledge of how all persons will respond to his love, then perhaps it is entirely fitting to speak of God's "trying" to save all persons. God hopes he will succeed, but perhaps he will not. Not even he knows. Moreover, if God cannot save all persons, perhaps he will be frustrated and his effort could eventually be judged a failure.

While this objection has a certain plausibility, I would argue nevertheless that such language is misleading at best when applied to God, even on the view that he has only general foreknowledge of future free choices. Recall that according to the view espoused by Geach and others, God has exhaustive knowledge of all possible choices humans could make and all possible courses the history of the world could take. Moreover, God knows how he would respond to any situation which might arise.

Because of this, nothing could happen to surprise God. He could never encounter unexpected obstacles or be at a loss as to how to respond to any situation. Consequently, much of what is implied in the idea of frustration could not apply to God. Similar difficulties attend the suggestion that God could fail. If God created with full knowledge of all possible courses the world could take, then presumably any of those possibilities would be acceptable for accomplishing his objectives.

This is not to say, of course, that all such possibilities would be *equally* acceptable to God. To the contrary, some of these surely include events and outcomes God would prefer not to happen. Even if God is prepared for all such events and outcomes, and has plans indexed to all of them, it could still be the case that his desires would not prevail at many specific points and his will for many persons would go unfulfilled. In this sense, it would be appropriate to say God could be frustrated.

I would hasten to reiterate, however, that any world which God would be prepared to accept would be a world which, overall, achieved his purposes. Any world which falls within this range would be a world which actualized sufficient value for God to accomplish his aims in creating. Even on a worst case scenario, in which the worst acceptable world were actualized, it would still be the case that the world as a whole would be such that God judged it good to create. In view of this, any talk of frustration as applied to God must be carefully qualified if it is not to be fundamentally misleading.

It is worth noting at this point that there are ways to avoid altogether the conclusion that God could be frustrated by those who freely refuse salvation. Richard Creel, who holds with Hick the view that God has only general foreknowledge, offers one such way in the following.

. . . I agree that God cares intensely that His will be fulfilled, but His will is not that we love Him; it is that we choose Him or not, and that, as a consequence, we become a part of His kingdom or not. In this sense God's will is always fulfilled. We always choose for Him or not. Therefore He suffers no frustration of His will. But does God want everyone to be in His kingdom, so that He grieves if even one person rejects it? No. He wants everyone in his kingdom who freely chooses it—and that He will get.[33]

Questions may be raised about Creel's claim that it is not God's will that we love him, as well as his claim that God does not sorrow over those who reject him, and I shall return to these in the next chapter. But I do think Creel's position represents a consistent option for those who accept the general view of foreknowledge but judge it inappropriate to think that God's will could be thwarted in any way whatsoever.

With respect to God's intention to save all persons, there is a further reason, given Hick's premises, why it would be wrong to say that God might fail. Since it is always possible for any sinner to repent, and not even God knows with certainty whether or not any given sinner will repent, it would *never* be true to say that God had failed to save that sinner. Talk of failure would only be appropriate if at some point the sinner was irreversibly damned. Since this point never comes according to Hick, there would never be ground for even suggesting the possibility of God's failing.

So it would be more accurate for Hick to say that God always *offers* sinners a chance to be saved, even into eternity. But strictly speaking, God does not "try" to save them, for this implies the possibility of failure, and as we have seen, this makes no sense at all, given Hick's position.

But to return to the point that nothing could surprise God, it is noteworthy that Hick himself gave eloquent expression to this idea. Indeed, Hick suggests that God had more than just a general foreknowledge of all possibilities when he created.

We must not, under the impact of our vision of the demonic, deify evil and dethrone God. . . . It cannot be unforeseen by the Creator or beyond His control. We must not suppose that God intended evil as a small domestic animal, and then was taken aback to find it growing into a great ravening beast! The creator to whom this could happen is not God. . . . We have in the end, then, both to recognize the essentially demonic nature of evil, and to maintain the sole ultimate sovereignty and omni-responsibility of God. . . . His decision to create the existing universe was the primary and necessary precondition for the occurrence of evil, all other conditions being contingent upon this, and He took His decision in awareness of all that would flow from it.[34]

Notice particularly the claim that God made the decision to create with awareness of all that *would* flow from his decision. This is stronger than the claim that God knew all that *could* flow from his decision to create. It implies that God had detailed foreknowledge of what actually would happen in the future course of the world.

Whether or not this was Hick's thought, I want to emphasize that if one takes this stronger view of divine foreknowledge, it makes no sense at all to say God would "try" to save all persons, or be a failure if he could not. To see this, suppose some possible world *W* includes the state of affairs *S* that human beings are free in the libertarian sense either to accept or reject God's grace. Suppose further that God knows with certainty that if he were to create *W*, some would never accept his grace. If this were so, God could not both create *W and* save all persons in it. It would be absurd to say God might try to do both, or that he would be a failure since he could not.

So if God chooses to create *W*, then he cannot save all persons in it without destroying their freedom. Furthermore, this would be perfectly consistent with the claim that God is omnipotent. It might be doubted whether it is consistent with God's perfect goodness to create such a world, but it is surely consistent with his omnipotence.

It must be emphasized that it does not follow that God is indifferent to those persons who will never receive grace since, strictly speaking, he does not "try" to save them. For we may coherently believe that God is willing to save these persons, and that he gives them a genuine opportunity to be saved, even if he knows they will reject it.

Indeed, we may properly say God regrets the fact that some in this world will not receive salvation. He truly wants them to be saved and is disappointed by the knowledge that they will not be. To say God *wants* to save such persons is significantly different from saying he tries to save them; and to say God is *disappointed* if he knows he cannot is likewise different from saying he is a failure on that account. The preferred terminology underscores the point that God truly desires to save such persons, while avoiding the suggestion that his omnipotence is threatened if he cannot.

It is important to underscore this point, for if God were not truly willing to save the lost, his goodness would surely be in doubt. If God did not provide a genuine opportunity for these persons to be saved, it would not be clear that they have chosen their fate and are truly responsible for it. Without such a genuine opportunity for salvation, it would make little sense to say they have rejected it.

Returning to Hick, as we have seen, his arguments in behalf of universalism are fraught with inconsistency and confusion. Before concluding this section, I want to suggest some moves Hick might take in order to achieve consistency.

First, if he is committed to the view that people are genuinely free in their relationship to God, and that future free actions are unknowable in principle, then he should not pretend that we can be confident that all will be saved. Universalism might turn out to be true, but if not even God can know that it will, surely none of us can.

Second, if Hick wants to stick with his original argument that universalism follows from God's perfect goodness and sovereignty, then he should be prepared to give up his view of freedom. He could do this in a number of ways. First, he could adopt a compatibilist view of freedom. If freedom and determinism are compatible, then I would agree with Hick that universalism is entailed by God's perfect goodness and sovereignty. Of course, if Hick were to make this move, he would have to change his view that there would be no point in God's creating finite beings without "genuine" freedom, and his whole theodicy would be undercut. Second, Hick could argue that a good God would not create beings who could go on resisting him forever. A good God would give us such a nature that this would be impossible. He would set the limits on our possible choices in such a way that we would not be able to resist forever. Given this assumption, again, universalism follows from God's being both perfectly good and omnipotent. But the argument rests heavily now on a certain claim about divine goodness. Third, Hick could hold that God has given human beings libertarian freedom, and that, so far as human nature is concerned, we could resist God forever. However, a good God would not allow anyone to resist his love forever. If any persons display obstinance to a certain point, God would simply override their freedom, and make them willing to accept salvation. Again, given this requirement for perfect goodness, universalism surely follows.

It is noteworthy that Origen, one of the first universalists, apparently took such a strategy. He admitted that there are those "whose conversion is in a certain degree demanded and extorted."[35] And it is similarly significant that Thomas Talbott, who argues that universalism is the only version of Christian theism which is even possibly true, makes the same sort of move. Talbott claims we have "every reason to believe that everlasting separation is the kind of evil that a loving God would prevent even if it meant interfering with human freedom in certain ways."[36]

A third option available to Hick would allow him to retain his argument that universalism follows from God's perfect goodness and omnipotence, and also maintain that persons are free in the libertarian sense. However, he would have to give up his belief that future free actions are unknowable in principle and accept the view that God has middle knowledge. If he were willing to do this, he could argue that a perfectly good God would only create those persons he knew would eventually receive grace. Again, universalism follows, but only by virtue of a certain stipulation about what is required for perfect goodness.

Indeed, what all these cases suggest is that the argument for universalism from God's goodness and omnipotence derives whatever plausibility it has from implicit but controversial assumptions about the nature of perfect goodness. The attribute of omnipotence actually plays a relatively minor role in the argument, particularly once it is clearly seen that if human beings are free in the libertarian sense, God might not be able to save everyone. So the real issue to be decided here is what is required for perfect goodness. And we shall turn to this in the next chapter.

V

I have argued that Calvinism and universalism share an important similarity in that both assume God can save anyone he will. Because God is omnipotent or sovereign, they say, he can bring about the free obedience of any creature. They disagree on the extent to which his goodness requires that he do so. The universalist holds that if God is good, he will want to win a free response of love and obedience from everyone. Therefore, all will be saved. The Calvinist, on the other hand, holds that God's will is to elicit such a response only from the elect. Because of his sovereign power, God can rightly ordain the rest of humanity to damnation.

I have also shown that both the Calvinist and the universalist slide into confusion in their effort to maintain both that God can save anyone, and that human beings are free. The Calvinist generally assumes a compatibilist account of freedom, but libertarian freedom slips in when he tries to avoid the unwelcome moral implications of his view of predestination. And libertarian freedom causes problems for the assumption that God can save anyone he will. By contrast, the universalist generally insists upon libertarian freedom. She runs into difficulty when trying to reconcile this with the claim that universalism follows necessarily from God's perfect goodness and power. If her commitment to universalism takes precedence, she may have to move in the direction of compatibilism or compromise her view of freedom when faced with the consequence that God might not be able to save everyone.

When libertarian freedom is consistently maintained, it will be recognized that God's ability to bring about certain states of affairs is contingent upon the choices of free creatures. In view of this, perhaps God cannot create a world in which everyone is saved, as the universalist supposes. Nor is it the case if some are lost, it follows that God is unwilling to save them. For God could be willing to save everyone, but unable to do so, while remaining properly omnipotent. It could be that he loves everyone and enables all of them to receive grace and be saved. If so, everyone would have a genuine opportunity to be saved. However, some might choose to continue in evil and be forever separated from God's love.

It is of the essence of the doctrine of hell that this possibility is actually realized in our world.

4

HELL AND DIVINE GOODNESS

I

Up until now, the issue of God's goodness has been largely in the background, although it has cast its shadow over our entire discussion. In the last chapter, important questions about divine goodness were constantly lurking in the neighborhood as we saw that it is possible, so far as omnipotence is concerned, that God cannot save all persons. Such questions can be delayed no longer, and I shall engage them directly in this chapter.

To feel the full force of the issues, we need to realize just what is involved in the claim that God is perfectly good. For a start, let us reflect on the following words of John Wesley.

> It is not written, "God is justice," or "God is truth:" (Although he is just and true in all of his ways:) But it is written, "God is love," love in the abstract, without bounds; and "there is no end of his goodness." His love extends even to those who neither love nor fear him. He is good, even to the evil and unthankful; yea, without any exception or limitation, to all the children of men. For "the Lord is loving" (or good) "to every man, and his mercy is over all his works."[1]

In emphasizing God's love and mercy, Wesley gave expression to a common Christian sensibility. The conviction that God is first and foremost a God of love is at the very heart of Christian faith.

What is more significant, for our purposes, is that Wesley identifies God's love with his goodness. This is noteworthy because perfect goodness can easily take on moralistic tones and be construed as a cold and impersonal attribute. It appears quite otherwise, however, in light of the notion that God's goodness is displayed in extending love and mercy to all creation. God wants all creatures to be happy,[2] and since happiness for persons is found only in relationship to himself, he wants all persons to accept salvation. God's goodness in this sense is sometimes called his moral goodness. The claim that God is morally good is usually understood by theists to imply that he always does what ought to be done. Moreover, God goes beyond what ought to be done in that he freely actualizes morally good states of affairs. However, it does not follow from this that God can ever fail to do what ought to be done, for according to many classical theologians, he is necessarily good. It is not possible for God to do evil.[3]

Of course, this is not the only way to understand God's goodness. Another important traditional idea is that God is supremely good in the metaphysical sense. That is to say, God is good by virtue of possessing properties of great intrinsic value. Indeed, God is the greatest possible being, and as such, is worthy of our worship. So God's metaphysical goodness is also crucial to the religious life.

But it remains true that it is God's moral goodness or volitional goodness (or, as Marilyn Adams has recently termed it, his "agent centered goodness"[4]) which typically takes center stage in Christian piety and devotion. It is the sort of goodness Wesley described which inspires love in human creatures: "We love because He first loved us."[5] This sort of goodness is relatively free of the arcane and controversial philosophical trappings generally associated with God's metaphysical goodness. It is intuitively grasped by ordinary believers, and if pressed, most would probably sooner compromise their belief in one or another element of God's metaphysical goodness, or in some other aspect of his nature, before they would compromise in any way their belief in his moral goodness, or his love. This is suggested by the popular appeal of certain religious books which depict God as all good, but as limited in power.

Given the religious and devotional importance of God's goodness, it is easy to see why the doctrine of eternal hell is so unsettling for many Christian believers. How is it even remotely possible to believe God is good in the sense expressed by Wesley while also believing that he has sovereign control over a world in which some persons will experience eternal misery? Can it make any sense at all to say God's love extends to such persons? Would a perfectly good God create a world in which he knew that some would be damned, or that some would *probably* be damned? Would God even create a world in which he knew it was *possible* that some would be eternally damned? Or would a perfectly good God prevent eternal damnation at any cost, even if it required him to override human freedom?

These questions take us back to our discussion of divine foreknowledge and remind us again that God's goodness cannot properly be considered in isolation from his other attributes. In our previous discussion, we considered views which hold that God has infallible specific foreknowledge of all future events as well as views which maintain that God has only general knowledge of the future. With respect to the first of these, I have already concluded that Calvinism is incompatible with any defensible account of God's goodness. However, we have yet to pursue the question of whether Molinism might provide a way of construing the doctrine of hell which is compatible with the conviction that God is perfectly good. Thus far, I have only suggested that Molinism does not provide an immediate solution to the sort of problems posed by Calvinism.

In what follows, I will subject Molinism to critical evaluation, and in the process I will develop a position on divine goodness which shows promise of resolving the moral problems in the traditional doctrine of hell. After responding to some objections against the account I develop, I will note how it can be employed in a general knowledge framework and discuss some relevant implications. Then I will turn to consider two further distinct issues which have a significant bearing on the fundamental question of whether any traditional doctrine of hell can be reconciled with the claim that God is perfectly good.

II

Let us proceed with our evaluation of Molinism by specifying why it does not provide an obvious solution to difficulties Calvinism faces. The problem with Molinism is not merely that God creates some person in circumstances in which he knows they will choose evil and be damned; rather, the difficulty is raised by some specific aspects of the claim that God has middle knowledge. Given this assumption, the possibility arises that some or all of these persons would choose right and be saved if they were put in different circumstances or were subject to different influences. Or perhaps some of these persons would have died in a state of grace[6] and been saved had they lived longer or not lived as long as they did.

In order to see these possibilities more clearly, let us reflect on some concrete examples. First, let us take the case of two persons who are born and raised in very different situations. One is born into a home in which he is deprived of both physical and emotional needs. He is never loved and receives virtually no religious instruction. Throughout his life, he is faced by a wide array of temptations and eventually he becomes a criminal and dies a violent death. The other, by contrast, is born into a loving family which provides for all his needs, including his emotional and spiritual needs. He is faithfully taught Christian precepts and becomes himself a devout believer. Suppose God knows the first would also have become a devout believer if he had been raised in the second person's circumstances.

Next, consider the case of two young women, both of whom have been taught the Christian faith, but have rejected it. Both are involved in an automobile accident in which one is killed while the other lives. Let us say the second is eventually converted and becomes a saintly person, whereas the first is damned. Suppose God knows the first would also have become a saintly person if she had lived to a normal age before dying.

Finally, let us think about Bertrand Russell's remarks on the notion that salvation and damnation may depend on fortuitous circumstances or events. This belief, Russell noted, motivated at least one very dubious practice.

> The Spaniards in Mexico and Peru used to baptize Indian infants and then immediately dash their brains out: by this means, they secured that these infants went to Heaven. No orthodox Christian can find any logical reason for condemning their actions, although all nowadays do.[7]

Leaving aside Russell's claim that an orthodox Christian has no good reason to condemn this practice, let us reflect on the larger implications of the case. What if God knows many of the slaughtered infants would have become wicked persons and died outside of grace if they had lived a full life span? Is their salvation really in some way secured by the fact that they were murdered before they had the chance to go astray?[8]

What all these cases suggest is that it is very odd, to say the least, to think that salvation and damnation might hinge in some way on such factors as the circumstances of one's birth or the time of one's death. If this is actually possible, it seems to raise doubts about the claim that God, in perfect goodness, desires to save all persons.

To bring this into focus, let us come back for a moment to Wesley's suggestive account of divine goodness. In a passage which has significant implications for our discussion, Welsey said that God's goodness is displayed most clearly

> in offering salvation to every creature, actually saving all that consent thereto, and doing for the rest all that infinite wisdom, almighty power, and boundless love can do, without forcing them to be saved, which would be to destroy the very nature that he had given them.[9]

So our question can be put like this: does it make any sense to say God does all he can to save all persons, short of destroying their freedom, if he allows some of them to be damned through unfavorable circumstances?

Let us zero in on this question by asking more specifically why it seems objectionable to think the circumstances of one's birth or the time of one's death might be a factor in his damnation. This is objectionable, I think, because it means some persons are at a distinct disadvantage with respect to the most important thing in life, namely, eternal salvation. Some persons have little or no chance to achieve ultimate happiness. If they had the opportunity others have, they would accept salvation, but since they do not, their fate is eternal misery. It seems intolerable that anyone should be at such a disadvantage, through no fault of their own, with respect to something of such significance.

It is noteworthy that Wesley struggled deeply with the fact that many persons in our world seem to have no real opportunity to receive salvation, due to their circumstances. He could not see how this could be compatible with his conviction that God's goodness extends to these persons. Indeed, he recognized this as a formidable objection against the Christian revelation.

Nothing is more sure than that "without holiness no man shall see the Lord." Why is it then that so vast a majority of mankind are, so far as we can judge, cut off from all means, all possibility of holiness, even from their mother's womb? For instance: what possibility is there that a Hottentot, a New Zealander, or an inhabitant of Nova Zembla, if he lives and dies there, should ever know what holiness means? Or consequently ever attain it? . . . From the time he comes into the world till he goes out of it again he seems to be under a dire necessity of living in all ungodliness and unrighteousness.

Wesley finally admitted this to be a mystery we cannot resolve. We caN only avoid the force of this objection against Christianity by "resolving all into the unsearchable wisdom of God, together with a deep conviction of our ignorance and inability to fathom his counsels."[10]

Wesley is no doubt correct that we cannot begin to fathom all the workings of divine providence. When dealing with this topic, reserve and modesty are very much in order. But when God's goodness is so severely challenged, it is desirable to do more than appeal to mystery, if at all possible.

Let us move in this direction by probing the implications of Wesley's claim that God is willing to do everything he can, short of destroying freedom, to save all persons. If this is entailed by God's perfect goodness, and I think it is, then it seems reasonable to suppose that God might somehow eliminate the disadvantages some have because of unfavorable circumstances. To eliminate the disadvantages would give all persons an equal opportunity to receive salvation. This would provide a solution to the difficulties in Molinism as well as an answer to Wesley's problem.

However, it is not a simple task to say in detail what may be involved in God's giving all persons an equal opportunity to receive salvation. As a rough approximation, let us consider the following. Suppose that for each created person there is some measure of grace N which represents the optimal amount of influence toward good which God can exercise on that person's will without destroying his freedom. What I am suggesting is that if God desires to save all persons, he will give to each person whatever is the optimal measure of grace for that person.

This measure of grace should not be conceived as a static, uniform given. Rather, it will differ in some respects from one individual person to another. What represents measure N for Jones may completely overwhelm Smith in such a way that his freedom is destroyed. Moreover, what is effective in influencing Smith toward good may only make Jones more resistant. So the even distribution of grace does not in any way entail treating all persons in just the same way. It means doing what is best for each individual to elicit, if possible, a positive response from him.

Another way of making this point is to say that God need not give everyone the *maximal* amount of grace which he can give without abrogating freedom. Some persons may respond to a lesser portion of grace. These persons need only to receive the minimally sufficient amount of grace, which would be that level of grace which would effectively dispose them to receive salvation. For these persons, the effective level of grace may fall far short of the level at which their freedom would be overridden.

It is also important to stress that optimal grace does not require the absence of all adversity and trial. Indeed, since the response of faith includes a moral dimension, a certain element of trial may be a necessary component of optimal grace. What is needed for grace to be optimal is the enablement and encouragement to respond positively to adversity, rather than simply the elimination of all adversity. Such grace enables one to respond with trust and humility rather than bitterness and anger. It compensates for the unfair disadvantages which some have had because of the excessive hardship they have faced. So the criminal described above did not lack optimal grace just because he had to face difficulty, but because the degree of difficulty seemed to put him at an overwhelming disadvantage so far as the opportunity to receive salvation is concerned.

With these qualifications on what is meant by "equal," I would say grace is distributed equally if grace of optimal measure is given to all persons and all are given full opportunity to make a decisive response to it, either positively or negatively. What is crucial here is the idea of a decisive response, but it is important to recognize that this is closely connected to the idea of an optimal measure of grace.

First, let us state more completely what a decisive response amounts to. I would propose that it is a settled response which is made by one fully informed of the Christian faith. Such a response would not be haphazard, superficial, or prone to change in shifting circumstances or with awareness of new information. Such a response could be described as a rooted disposition. As such, it normally would not be achieved in a moment, but rather only through a longer series of choices. Thus, one's initial choices might be against God and the good, but in the long run one might come to love God in a settled way. What is decisive is not one's initial choices, but the settled disposition one ultimately acquires.

Given God's desire to save all persons, a decisive negative response makes sense only in light of the idea of optimal grace. That is to say, a negative response to God is decisive only if one persists in rejecting God in the most favorable circumstances. Only then is it clear that one has rejected God in a settled way with true understanding.

Another way of making this point is to say that a negative disposition to God is decisive only if it has been formed by a deliberate rejection of God's grace. Such a disposition would not be decisive if it were formed by other factors or influences. Optimal grace may overcome a negative disposition to God which is due to contingent circumstances, but it would not help a person whose negative reaction to God was shaped precisely by the persistent refusal of grace.

Thus, in our case of the two young women, I am inclined to say the one killed had not decisively rejected God. Although her initial response to grace was negative, she would have become a saintly person had she lived longer. This suggests that her initial negative reaction to God was not really a settled response. If God knows this, it may be the case that God will give her the grace at the moment of death to begin to become what she would have become if she had not died. Further spiritual growth could occur after death.[11] The same is true of our person born into a life of deprivation. His life of crime does not constitute a decisive rejection of God since he has not rejected God in the most favorable circumstances, and would, moreover, have become a devout believer in different circumstances. God, we may assume, could bring about the appropriate favorable circumstances during the passage of death, thereby making up for his previous deprivation.[12] Then he could make a fully decisive response to God. Something like this, I think, would represent grace of measure N for this person.

A similar sort of move will resolve Wesley's problem. The persons he is concerned about have probably not rejected God in a decisive way since they have never even heard the Christian message, let alone understood it. It does not seem likely that God would allow such persons to be damned without a full opportunity to receive salvation, particularly if he knows some of these persons would have responded in a positive way if given the chance. It is reasonable to think God will somehow provide these persons with as much opportunity to be saved as anyone else has had.[13]

Indeed, it is hard to avoid a conclusion like this if one believes God is good in the sense described by Wesley. Unless one thinks there is some reason why God cannot make up for the disadvantages some have, it seems to follow from his perfect goodness that he will do so.

But perhaps there are good reasons why God cannot eliminate all such disadvantages and give all an optimal measure of grace. In the first place, perhaps I have assumed too easily that God could make up for previous deprivation and bring about the "appropriate favorable circumstances" in which a person would receive grace. Surely this could not be achieved at the drop of a hat, and perhaps some effects of deprivation simply cannot ever be eliminated. Perhaps some persons *would have* responded positively to grace in certain favorable circumstances, but they have become so hardened and embittered by their experiences in the actual world that nothing can be done now or in the future to elicit a positive response from them. The fact that our criminal would have become a devout believer in some feasible world does not entail that God can reach him in the actual world.

In response to this, I would argue that my assumption that God could make up for any previous deprivation is a reasonable one, given God's perfect love and insight into human nature. It may take considerable time for God to restore an embittered person to a condition in which he would accept grace, so this could not always, if ever, be achieved at the drop of a hat. But given God's unlimited resources of love and understanding, I think it is plausible to assume he could eventually accomplish this.

Yet another problem remains, however, for the claim that God could give all persons optimal grace. Isn't it possible that the giving of optimal grace to one person may entail giving less than optimal grace to another? For instance, could it not be the case that the best thing God can do to move, say, Luther to repentance is to withhold grace from Erasmus, allowing him to ruin his life through sin and folly? Observing the ruin of Erasmus may be the best way, if not the only way, of impressing upon Luther his need for God. In the end then, God cannot avoid distributing grace unequally.

This is a troubling suggestion which I find difficult to assess. On the one hand, there is no denying that a negative example can be a powerful impetus to do good. But on the other hand, it is doubtful whether optimal grace for anyone necessarily includes such negative inspiration. Since one of the primary purposes of God's grace is to make us loving persons who desire the welfare of others, it is hard to see how the ruin of someone could be essential for anyone to receive such grace.

But suppose it is nevertheless true that Luther can be moved to repent only by observing the ruin of Erasmus. It does not follow from this that Erasmus must finally be damned. For God could still, at the time of death, give Erasmus the grace withheld during this life. Thus, Luther could be moved to repent by the negative example of Erasmus, but Erasmus could ultimately be given the grace and opportunity to respond as he would have responded had he received more grace in this life. In the end, both Luther and Erasmus could receive optimal grace and be saved.

Now I readily admit that my solutions to these problems are far from conclusive. However, I want to suggest that both problems gain much of their force from the assumption that grace cannot extend beyond the boundary of this present life. On this assumption, the idea that grace is unevenly distributed is fairly compelling. If there can be no opportunity to receive grace at or beyond the point of death, then it seems most likely that grace is not, and perhaps cannot be, optimally bestowed on all persons. But if God can extend grace beyond this life, it can be plausibly held that he will do so, until all have had full opportunity to receive it.

Of course, the assumption that the opportunity to receive grace can extend beyond this life is also controversial. But if it is granted, I think the problems I have noted can be satisfactorily addressed, and we may reasonably maintain that God can and will make up for the disadvantages pertaining to salvation which some have in this life.

If we cannot maintain this, we cannot sustain the claim that God does everything possible to save all persons, short of destroying anyone's freedom. If God does less for some persons to bring about their salvation, he does not fully desire their happiness. And if there are some persons whose happiness God does not fully desire, his perfect goodness is compromised. So God's perfect goodness does seem to entail that he fully desires the salvation of all persons and will therefore give all an optimal measure of grace.

But as I have already indicated, it is possible that some would not respond favorably to even an optimal measure of grace, and would instead reject God in a decisive way. So I want to suggest as a preliminary conclusion that the account which I have been sketching may provide a way to maintain both that God is perfectly good and that some will be eternally damned. Without the amendments I have proposed, I do not think Molinism provides an adequate account of God's goodness and desire to save all persons. But if God does everything he can to save all persons, short of destroying anyone's freedom, it may be that God can, consistent with perfect goodness, create some persons knowing they will never act in accordance with grace.

I want to emphasize, however, that it can be plausibly held that God need not have middle knowledge or absolute foreknowledge in order to know that a person's response to grace is decisive. By knowing a person's history, intentions, and so on, God could know a person's response was fully informed and deliberate. He could know when a person's character was so formed by his choices that in all likelihood it would never change. In such a case, I think we could fairly say God knows that person's response to grace is decisive.

III

There are other objections which are likely to be raised against the view of divine goodness which I have defended. Some of these are philosophical in nature, whereas others are more theological.

First, the question may be asked why anyone should endeavor now to love God and do good if there may be further opportunity at death or after death to receive salvation. If God's perfect goodness entails that all receive an equal chance to be saved, doesn't this undercut the sense of urgency normally associated with seeking salvation. Doesn't it encourage presumption to think there may be a further chance to be saved at the time of death?

In reply to this, I would emphasize that those who may be given further chance after death to receive salvation are given no more than the opportunity to make a *decisive* choice either to accept or reject God's will. It is not as if God turns the tables by finally giving them *more* than is given to others. Rather, the idea is that God would give these persons no more and no less than he has given many others, namely, just that measure of grace best suited to win a free favorable response to his love. Then they could make the decisive choice which they never made in this life due to the fact that they never really understood the Christian message or were otherwise deprived in ways which prevented them from making a settled choice on the matter.

This does not, however, provide any ground for anyone to think his present choices do not count. Anyone who understands the argument I have presented is probably fairly well informed on religious matters. Such persons would not likely be among those who do not understand the Christian message. If such persons continue to reject salvation on the presumption that they can repent later, it may well be that they are forming, by that very attitude, a settled disposition to prefer their will to God's. At the very least, this may make it much more difficult for them to come to accept God's will.

A second objection, related to the first, is that if God's goodness entails what I have argued, there is no adequate motive for Christian missions. If God will eventually provide all people an equal opportunity for salvation, there is no good reason to spend the effort and money required to take the gospel around the world. On this view, missionaries do not convert people who would otherwise be lost. If God will somehow ensure that all persons receive an optimal measure of grace, then anyone who would be converted through the efforts of missionaries will be saved anyway.

Now I will readily admit that much mission work has been largely motivated by the belief that all persons who do not hear and receive the gospel in this life will be lost. It has been assumed, in other words, that all persons will not have equal chance to be saved, and it is up to us to do what we can to ensure that as many as possible have at least some chance.

However, it does not follow that there is no other adequate motive or rationale for mission work. Consider the following analogy. Suppose we knew of a group of people who lacked adequate food and were consequently suffering the pain of malnutrition. But we also knew that eventually, after several years, these people would be provided all the food they need. In the meantime they suffer from perpetual hunger.

It seems clear to me that we would have good reason to take food to those people immediately, even if we knew that none of them would die if we did not. It would be good to relieve their hunger as soon as possible and to participate in the joy of seeing others experience fulfillment and satisfaction such as they have never known. Similarly, there is good reason to take the Christian message around the world now, even if we think God will ensure all persons a full opportunity to receive salvation, regardless of what we do. If the Christian message is crucial for human fulfillment and happiness, it is good for all persons to hear that message as soon as possible. Those who have experienced fulfillment through the Christian faith and are grateful for it have ample motivation to obey Christ's command to take the gospel to all nations, even if they do not assume that all those who do not hear the gospel in this life will be lost.

Moreover, this account of why Christians should engage in missions avoids a difficult problem in the traditional view, namely, that it entails the unacceptable conclusion that some persons may be damned largely because of the failure or disobedience of others. According to that view, if Christians fail in the task of evangelism and missions, many persons will consequently be damned, who would otherwise be saved, for they will die without hearing the gospel. This point cannot be dismissed by claiming that such persons are damned solely because of sins they personally have committed. If it is true that they would have repented if they had heard the gospel, and the only reason they did not hear it is because Christians failed in their responsibility to evangelize them, then the conclusion is inescapable that the failure of others contributes largely to their damnation. I would argue that this implication is unacceptable if we take seriously the perfect justice of God, not to mention his goodness. It accords better with divine justice to hold that none will be damned because of the failure of others. This follows, of course, if God will ensure that all persons receive a full opportunity to receive salvation.

Third, it might be argued that God's perfect goodness can be maintained in a Molinist framework without the hypothesis that God will give all persons an equal opportunity to be saved. William Lane Craig, for instance, suggests that:

> it is possible that God in his providence so arranged the world that those who never in fact hear the gospel are persons who would not respond if they did hear it. God brings the gospel to all those who he knows will respond to it if they hear it. . . . No one who would respond if he heard it will be lost.[14]

If this were true, no one would be lost because of unfavorable circumstances or disadvantages. Those who have little or no chance to accept the Christian message are persons who would not respond favorably no matter how much opportunity they had.

I want to emphasize that initially Craig suggests this as nothing more than a *possibility*. His primary concern is to show that there is no inconsistency in believing the following two propositions.

1. God is omniscient, omnipotent, and omnibenevolent.
2. Some persons do not receive Christ and are damned.

Following the model of Plantinga's "free will defense," Craig proposes the following as a proposition which is consistent with (1) and entails (2).

3. God has actualized a world containing an optimal balance between saved and unsaved, and those who are unsaved suffer from transworld damnation.[15]

"Those who are unsaved" are for Craig those who do not receive the gospel in this life and are consequently lost. Such persons suffer from "transworld damnation" which means they would not receive the gospel in any feasible world in which they exist. Put in terms of the passage cited above, those who never hear the gospel, but who suffer from transworld damnation, would not respond to the gospel if they did hear it. And it is possible that God in his providence has so arranged things that all those who never hear the gospel suffer from transworld damnation.

So long as Craig's proposal is taken only as an account of what is possible, I find no fault with it. Unfortunately, however, he has ventured the further claim that he finds his account to be "quite plausible not only as a defense, but also as a soteriological theodicy."[16] In other words, it deserves consideration as a description of what is probably true as well as possibly true. Presented in these terms, I find it extremely implausible. This account could not be disproved, of course, even if offered as a sober proposal about what is actually the case, but it is exceedingly hard to entertain seriously the notion that all the persons who lived and died in countries the gospel did not reach for centuries would have rejected it if they had heard it. So I think something like the hypothesis I have proposed is necessary if we are concerned to provide a serious and credible account of how God's perfect goodness is compatible with the fact that some persons have little or no opportunity to hear the gospel in this life.

It is worth noting that Craig's proposition can be read in such a way that it agrees with the view I have defended. Read like this, the "unsaved" would refer to those persons who have decisively rejected, or will decisively reject God's grace, offered in optimal conditions, either in this life or after death. On this definition, it remains true that the unsaved suffer from transworld damnation. It follows that those who suffer from transworld damnation and die without hearing the gospel would have rejected it if they had heard it, but it does not follow that those who die without hearing the gospel suffer from transworld damnation.[17]

Fourth, it may be argued that my response to the previous two objections points up another problem with the traditional doctrine of hell, namely, that there is something objectionable in the whole idea that Christian missions are even necessary. More specifically, why is it necessary for people to believe in Jesus, or accept the Christian gospel, whether in this world or the next, in order to be saved? Isn't it implausible, if not preposterous, to think that specific beliefs about a person could be required for salvation?

The answer to these questions depends entirely upon whether or not the classic Christian claims about Jesus are true. This is not, of course, the place to defend those claims. It is worth noting, however, that my account of optimal grace entails the notion that all persons will receive a revelation of who Jesus is, and what he has done for our salvation, which is fully adequate to enable a deliberate response to him. Now if classic Christian claims about Jesus are true, we can make sense of why belief in Christ, as traditionally understood, is necessary for salvation.

To begin, it must be remembered that the very essence of salvation is being restored to a right relationship to God. If Jesus was, and is, God the Son who became incarnate for our salvation, it is not hard to see why he must be acknowledged if we are to enjoy a right relationship with God. It would, in the first place, constitute a basic failure in honesty to decline to acknowledge Jesus as God if it were clearly revealed to one that that is who he is. Moreover, it would involve a failure to be properly grateful for what Jesus did on our behalf if it were clearly revealed that he became incarnate and died to atone for our sins.

These points can be amplified by noting explicitly that our beliefs are tied up closely with our actions, feelings, and attitudes. Swinburne's comment is apt.

> If you think God walked on Earth, you are likely to have a different kind of reverence for him than if you think of him merely as a philosopher's first principle; and also a different kind of reverence for men of whom God became one.[18]

Traditional belief in Christ is consequently not a mere theoretical commitment, but also a matter of deep devotional and practical significance. The belief required is not an arbitrary confession, but an appropriate response of acknowledgment, gratitude, and worship for who God is and what he has done to secure our salvation.

Another objection to the account I have defended goes like this: if God's perfect goodness entails that he will give all persons an optimal measure of grace, then in reality, the concept of grace has been eliminated. If God is necessarily perfectly good, then it is a matter of necessity that such grace be granted to all. And if it is a matter of necessity, it is not truly grace, for grace is by definition something which God freely bestows.

It is certainly true that an emphasis on divine freedom has been central in many traditional accounts of grace. Calvinism, of course, is the clearest example of this with its doctrine that God bestows or withholds grace as he will. The freedom of grace is thus bound up with its unequal distribution. As Calvin put it: "the very inequality of [God's] grace proves that it is free."[19] Molina held a similar view.

> God does not provide for all human beings and angels equally or in the same way, with regard to either supernatural or natural gifts, but rather decides to distribute the gifts of His mercy as He pleases, though no one is ever deprived of what is necessary. . . . [20]

I want to argue, however, that what is essential to the notion of grace is not that it is bestowed or withheld at will, but that it is undeserved. The idea that grace is freely bestowed is easily run together with the idea that it is undeserved. That is to say, it is easy to think that because none of us deserves grace, God can give it to whomever he will, overlooking the rest.

However, I think it is possible to maintain the lack of human desert without holding that God is free to withhold grace from anyone once that person is created. To see this, let us consider a parental analogy. Suppose a father has two children, both of whom go against his wishes by living reckless lives. Eventually both become addicted to drugs and require rehabilitation. They request help from their father, and since he has ample means, he gladly pays for their rehabilitation. Later, however, both revert to their old lifestyle and again become addicted and need rehabilitation. This happens several times. Suppose the father knows somehow that if he rehabilitates them one more time, they will gratefully get their lives in order and become responsible persons. But suppose he decides to rehabilitate only one of his children, leaving the other in a state of lifelong drug addiction and misery.

How would we judge this case? I think we would say that neither of the children deserved their father's help. He did not owe it to them to rehabilitate them over and over. However, if the father knows his children would go right if he were to rehabilitate them one more time, then I think we would doubt his love for his children if he declined to do so, especially if he has ample means. Moreover, we would think him a better person if he were to rehabilitate both, rather than only one. He would not be a perfectly good father if he left one of his children in a state of misery if he could help it.

In the same way, I do not think God's perfect goodness can be maintained if it is held that God withholds grace from some, or distributes grace unevenly in such a way that some are damned who would otherwise be saved. God's nature as a perfectly good being is such that he necessarily gives all people an equal opportunity to be saved. This does not destroy the notion of grace, however, for it remains true that we do not deserve salvation. It is still true that the ultimate ground of salvation lies in what God is, not in what we are.

There is, moreover, still an important element of freedom in grace. God did not create necessarily, but freely. Praise and gratitude are due to God since his free choice to create each being to whom he will then give optimal grace is what makes possible the salvation and eternal happiness of each of us.

Sixth, it might be suggested that perhaps God cannot extend grace to persons at the time of death, or after death, without destroying their freedom. After death God's reality may be so evident that it would be impossible to make a free response to him. In the face of his majesty and power, persons would feel compelled to submit out of fear. Such a reaction would not be out of faith and love so it would not count as genuine acceptance of grace and commitment to his will.

In response to this, I see no reason to assume God's existence must be more evident after death than it is now. Surely God could reveal himself only to such an extent as would enable a free response. Perhaps God may even continue to use human creatures as messengers on his behalf. The situation after death may be similar to this life in the sense that persons may learn about God from their fellow humans and respond in faith to what they learn.

A seventh objection can be put as follows: if God knows some persons will not respond to grace, even when bestowed in an optimal way, then he should not create those persons at all. If God creates such persons, there is still a problem about God's goodness similar to the problem in Molinism. It is not enough for God to give an equal portion of grace to such persons. The problem lies precisely in the claim that God creates such persons at all. A perfectly good God would create only those persons he knows will eventually accept grace.

This is a serious difficulty which cannot easily be resolved. However, it is open to rebuttal insofar as it assumes God could have created only persons who would accept grace. It is possible God could not have, particularly if the world he creates is populated with many persons. As Craig has pointed out, God perhaps could have created a world in which none would be lost if it contained only a few people. But it could be that God's desire is that great multitudes experience salvation. And surely, Craig argues, God could rightfully prefer a world in which many are saved even if many are lost over a world in which only a handful are saved and nobody lost.[21]

This is not to say that God could do nothing to minimize the number of the damned. God could use middle knowledge to choose out of all creatable or feasible worlds a world in which he knows many will be saved and in which the fewest number of persons are lost. (Let us assume for the moment, for the sake of simplicity, that all worlds contain the same number of people).

It is important to emphasize that no one would be lost in this world who would be saved in some other feasible world. If there is some feasible world in which a person will be saved, this means there is some measure of grace to which that person will freely respond. And God will give that person that measure of grace since it follows from God's perfect goodness that all persons are given an optimal portion of grace. Those who are damned, on the other hand, would be damned in every feasible world *in which they exist*. They would not respond in a positive way to any grace which God might offer. However, some who are damned in this world might not be damned in some other feasible worlds simply because they do not exist in those worlds. And our freedom with respect to procreation may partly determine which persons exist in which worlds.

However, it might be argued that there is still something objectionable in God's creating persons he knows will be damned, even if he creates as few such persons as he can. For those who are damned seem to be a sacrifice in behalf of the saved. That is to say, God is willing to sacrifice the lost in order to achieve his purpose of having a number of persons who accept his will and are saved.[22]

While this argument has a certain amount of initial force, I think it is largely mitigated if it is true, as I have argued, that the damned are given every opportunity to be saved. In view of this, it is not the case that the damned are "sacrificed" against their will. It is not like the case of a general in battle who must sacrifice some of his men in order to save the rest. In this situation, those who die in battle would presumably prefer to live, but do not have that option. Some *have* to die and they are the unfortunate ones who do.

However, since God gives all persons an optimal measure of grace, no one has to be lost. To the contrary, all could be saved, and if any are not, it is due to the fact that they have persisted in the choice to resist God's grace. So if they are "sacrifices," they are sacrifices of an unusual sort. They willingly and persistently choose their role. Consequently, it is hard to see how their damnation can serve as a decisive objection to God's perfect goodness.

One other issue a should be addressed before concluding this section. It might be argued that it is not enough for a perfectly good God to minimize the *number* of the damned; he would also have limits as to the *proportion* of persons damned. For instance, if God had the choice of creating a world of one million persons in which fifty percent would be lost or a world of ten million in which ten percent would be lost, he might prefer the latter world even though a greater number would be lost in it. The former world might be unacceptable because the proportion of persons lost is too high. In the same vein, if God knew that in every world with free creatures which he could create, at least ninety percent would be damned, he would simply forgo creating a world with free creatures.

Now as soon as this issue is raised, it will be apparent that it has no clear answer. Intuitions become extremely hazy when we ask what proportion of persons a perfectly good God would be willing to lose in order to create a world with free creatures. The question may seem at least somewhat amenable to answer if we think of it in terms of a temporal analogy. For instance, if we think again of a general who may have to lose some men in battle, it may seem tolerable to lose ten percent, but not sixty percent. But when we contemplate persons being eternally damned, no percentage seems *more* tolerable than another. Whatever the number, there is, in a sense, infinite loss, so it seems incongruous to quantify and compare it in any way. On the other hand, if the lost have rejected optimal grace and have fully chosen their fate, it is not obvious that any proportion is incompatible with God's perfect goodness, assuming God would keep that proportion to a minimum.

But again, I confess that my intuitions, at least, are very hazy at this point. I do not see any prospects for our determining by our own lights what proportion of persons a perfectly good God would judge it tolerable to lose. If there is such a specific proportion or number beyond which a perfectly good God would not go, only God could know it unless he chose to reveal it.

IV

I want briefly to return to the view that God's foreknowledge of the future is only general as opposed to specific and infallible. I have suggested that this view is not exempt from the sort of moral problems normally associated with the absolute foreknowledge view. In this chapter, I have developed an account of God's perfect goodness, assuming a broadly Molinist conception of absolute foreknowledge, which is compatible with some being eternally damned. The question now is whether this account of divine goodness can be adapted to resolve the moral problems of the general foreknowledge view.

I believe it can. The key idea, again, is the notion that God does everything he can to save all persons, short of destroying their freedom. The main difference is that God does not have the advantage of middle knowledge to help him create a world in which the number or proportion of the damned is kept at a minimum. However, God could still know all persons and their needs well enough to give all an optimal measure of grace and thereby save as many persons as possible.

But without absolute foreknowledge, God could not have known, prior to creation, how many persons would receive grace. At best, God could have known only what percentage of persons would *likely* go right, based on his knowledge of human nature. But it would be at least theoretically possible, assuming that persons can reject God decisively, that all would be lost. And on the other hand, all persons might eventually receive salvation. Without absolute foreknowledge, it seems that God must have been prepared for either possibility. The latter possibility, of course, would pose no problem for a perfectly good God. But what about the former? Could a perfectly good God allow all persons to be damned? Would such a God create a world in which this was even a possibility?

This raises again the issue of proportion. If a perfectly good God could not allow more than a certain proportion or number of persons to be damned, then God would be required to risk his perfect goodness if he decided to create a world of free creatures. There would be a chance, however slight, that more persons would decisively reject grace than he could allow, while maintaining his perfect moral character. In view of this, presumably God would be prepared to do whatever necessary to prevent this from happening.

The question is, what could God do? An answer which comes easily to mind is that God could override the freedom of some persons by making them willing to accept grace, in order to secure the salvation of the proportion needed to maintain perfect goodness. But this suggestion may seem absurd, once it is articulated. At best, it surely raises further questions.

For instance, *which* persons should God make willing to receive grace? Furthermore, if God is finally willing to override the freedom of *some* in order to maintain perfect goodness, then why shouldn't he be willing to do this for all those who persist in rejecting grace? For if God is willing to interfere with our freedom, it seems more plausible to accept universalism than the notion that God would do so only to keep the number of the saved at a certain proportion.

Indeed, this line of thought suggests that God need not be able to save any fixed percentage of persons in order to be perfectly good. His perfect goodness consists essentially in the fact that he saves the highest number or proportion he can, while giving all persons an optimal measure of grace. Construed in this way, God's goodness is in no way dependent upon his ability to save a particular percentage of free persons. No matter how many persons reject grace, God's perfect goodness remains secure. Consequently, a perfectly good God could create a world knowing it was at least possible that none of the persons in it would avail themselves of grace.

Now this is a difficult conclusion to embrace, but it must be pointed out that the alternative may be that no created persons would receive, or have the chance to receive the supreme creaturely happiness given to those who freely accept grace. If a perfectly good God would not take the risk that all would be lost, he might have to forgo creating a world with free creatures. The same is true if a certain proportion must be saved. If God could not take the risk that even a great majority may reject grace, then the great good of supreme happiness for some persons, whatever the number, would have to be forgone. It is not at all evident that this alternative is preferable to creating a world of free creatures, who have a full opportunity to receive eternal happiness, even if many of them are damned in the end.

This argument may have to be qualified on the assumption that God has middle knowledge. If God knew with certainty that *none* of the persons in worlds he could create would accept grace, then surely God would not create a world with free persons. But beyond this, it is not clear that any particular number or percentage must accept grace if God is to be perfectly good. Even if some accept eternal happiness, this is a great enough good to justify God's creation of free persons. However, the point for emphasis is that what is required for perfect goodness may differ according to whether or not God has middle knowledge. If he does, then he could not create a world in which all are damned; if he does not, he could.[23]

V

Before concluding this chapter, I want to raise two other issues which bear on the question of whether the doctrine of eternal hell is compatible with God's perfect goodness. First, I want to return to the suggestion that God would, if necessary, interfere with our freedom in order to prevent anyone from being damned. Thomas Talbott defends this claim against Richard Swinburne who has argued that: "Free will is a good thing, and for God to override it for whatever cause is to all appearances a bad thing."[24]

In the next chapter I will respond in detail to Talbott's view, so for now I will give only my short answer. The heart of the difference between Swinburne and Talbott depends upon the nature, and ultimately the value, of human freedom. Swinburne seems to place more value on freedom than does Talbott, since he does not think it should be overridden, even to prevent someone from being damned. Since this dispute involves a basic value judgment, it must be recognized that there is no simple way to resolve it, and indeed, it may represent a ground-level difference of intuition. In view of this, it will be evident that Talbott's claim that God would interfere with freedom in order to prevent anyone from being damned rests upon a highly controversial value judgment. Consequently, it will hardly serve as an authoritative account of what is required for perfect goodness.

The second issue I want to address must be dealt with at more length. This concerns the often-repeated argument that if some persons are eternally damned, a fully good God could not be perfectly happy. His joy would be forever marred if some of his creatures completely rejected grace. As Bertrand Brasnett put it, God "asks for the love of men and sorrows till he finds it."[25] If this is so, God must experience sorrow so long as there are some persons who do not love him.

The idea that God could be made to suffer or experience sorrow would have been rejected, of course, by most classical theologians. The predominant view has been that God is impassible. That is to say, God eternally experiences perfect bliss, and nothing that goes on in the world disturbs or affects his feelings in any way. In recent times, the doctrine of impassibility has been challenged, most notably by process theologians, but also by more orthodox theologians and philosophers.[26]

This issue is a difficult one to negotiate, for there are serious problems to be faced, no matter which view one takes. If one rejects the claim that God suffers pain or sorrow when his creatures reject him, one may end up with a God who is callous and indifferent. Such a God hardly seems to be a morally good being in any meaningful sense of the word. As an example of this tendency, consider Peter Geach's memorable words: "For God a billion rational creatures are as dust in the balance; if a billion perish, God suffers no loss, who can create what he wills with no effort or cost by merely thinking of it."[27]

On the other hand, if one insists that God does indeed suffer, one runs the risk of depicting God as an emotional hostage to recalcitrant sinners. Richard Creel makes this point in a vivid way by imagining how Friedrich Nietzsche might react to the idea of a suffering God.

> I can see Nietzsche saying with a grin, "Ahhh, so the old boy is real after all. This is even better! I may not be able to kill him, but I can make him damn well sorry he ever created me. . . .

"What if he casts me into hell for my mockery? If he does, then he will know that he has lost and I have won; remember, he loves me and must eternally grieve for me in my eternal damnation. And I in hell will continue with words and gestures of contempt and obscenity to remind him that he has lost and therefore is contemptible—that he could neither win my heart nor subdue my disdain . . . ."[28]

This is, as Creel argues, an unworthy conception of God. We should not imagine that God is in any way vulnerable to emotional manipulation.

So the Christian theologian is faced with a dilemma when considering the question of whether or not God suffers when human beings reject his love or suffer in other ways. Not surprisingly, there have been a number of efforts to resolve this dilemma by arguing that there is no incompatibility in holding both that God is perfectly blissful and that he suffers for/with us. Creel's verdict on such attempts is that they engage in double-talk and implicitly deny that God really suffers.[29]

Creel meets this dilemma by claiming that God's will for us is only that we freely choose either for or against his kingdom. God's will is not that we love him, so he experiences no sorrow or pain if we do not. God has created us not for himself, but for freedom, so it is a matter of indifference to him whether or not we choose his kingdom.

Were God to pine away over those who reject his kingdom, he would be as immature as a jilted lover who pines over what could have been if only the beloved had chosen differently, and who runs after the beloved making demeaning efforts to win her back. Such feelings and behaviour are not realistic or mature, nor do they respect the freedom and dignity of the beloved. They do not recognize that the beloved has freely chosen to be someone who does not pursue a romantic relationship with the lover, and they do not recognize the right of the beloved to make such a choice and have it accepted and respected by the lover.[30]

Creel's position successfully avoids the notion that God might be frustrated or vulnerable to emotional blackmail. However, I think he pays too high a price for this benefit. His claim that God created us for freedom rather than for himself raises questions as to whether God really loves us. It is essential to traditional Christian belief that those who accept God's kingdom will be much happier than those who do not. So if God has no real preference whether or not we accept his kingdom, it seems he does not care whether or not we are really happy. And if God does not care about our happiness, he does not really love us, in which case he is not perfectly good.

That Creel does not recognize the force of these points is indicated by his analogy of the jilted lover. There is a very important difference between God and the jilted lover Creel describes. The difference hinges on the fact that the beloved may be just as happy, or even happier, by pursuing romantic involvement with someone other than the lover. If the lover truly loves the beloved, if he truly wants what is best for her, then he can accept her choice and wish her well. But on the other hand, those who reject God and his kingdom cannot be just as happy or even happier than they would be if they chose to be a part of his kingdom. Even if the damned get what they want—as I shall argue later—and consequently experience some perverse sense of satisfaction, they still are not truly happy. So while God may accept and respect their choice, he must do so knowing they have forfeited what is best for them, for they cannot experience genuine fulfillment and happiness without accepting his love. Consequently, God cannot be perfectly good unless he wants all persons to accept his love and be members of his kingdom.

Now the question is whether we can maintain this view without entailing that God's happiness depends upon the choices of his creatures. Could God's bliss be sufficiently resilient that it could be compatible with an element of suffering over his children who fail to receive happiness? I want to suggest that it could be.

Let us consider this possibility by thinking again about Creel's position. Another way of stating my objection to his view is to say that God does not seem to have the right attitude toward his creatures if it is a matter of indifference to him whether or not they accept his kingdom. His attitude toward their loss of happiness does not seem appropriate to a perfectly good being. If he loves his human creatures, he should view their loss of happiness and fulfillment with something like a sense of regret.[31]

Perhaps the element of suffering which God experiences is an attitude of regret toward the loss of happiness by those who refuse his love. Conceived in this way, God's suffering is not a feeling which could dominate the divine consciousness. It is rather a moral attitude, a certain way of thinking about loved ones who have experienced great loss.

The very fact that God's attitude of regret is a moral attitude is what makes it impossible that God should be vulnerable to emotional manipulation in the manner Creel depicts. If God could become an emotional hostage to creatures who reject his love, then evil could prevail over perfect goodness. It is because God maintains a perfect moral attitude that he could not allow this to occur.

This means that God's perfect happiness, like his perfect goodness, does not depend in any way upon human choice. God views rejection with an attitude of regret because he *wants* human beings to be happy for *their own* sake. But he does not *need* them to be happy for *his* sake.

It may be objected that surely God would be happier if he did not have to view anything with an attitude of regret. And if so, God cannot be perfectly happy unless all are saved. Perfect happiness must be such that God could not be happier.

In response to this, I would agree that God's perfect happiness must be such that he could not be happier. However, I would suggest that perfect happiness may not conform to our *a priori* expectations. It may be that we conceive as perfect a description of happiness which does not include any element of suffering. But such happiness may not be an option, even for God, and thus, may not be the measure of perfection. Perfect happiness may be a more complex matter.

Maybe it is the case that God's only alternative to creating a world in which some are damned was to forgo creating any free creatures at all. Perhaps God would also have experienced regret if he had forgone creating a world of creatures who could respond to his love and enjoy a relationship with him. Perhaps God's regret in this case would have been greater than the regret he has over those who reject his kingdom.

If so, God's perfect happiness may inevitably include an element of suffering, or at least regret. Since God's happiness is the greatest actual happiness, accounts of perfect happiness which exclude all suffering may be conceivable, but, strictly speaking, unrealizable.

Incidentally, the view I have been sketching may also provide a solution to another problem closely related to the one we have been considering. The problem concerns the question of how those who are saved could be truly happy if they know that some of their fellow created persons are eternally damned. This problem, like the one we have been considering, has been a stock objection against traditional accounts of hell for some time. Friedrich Schleiermacher, for instance, stated the argument as follows.

> Now if we attribute to the blessed a knowledge of the state of the damned, it cannot be a knowledge unmixed with sympathy. If the perfecting of our nature is not to move backwards, sympathy must be such as to embrace the whole human race, and when extended to the damned must of necessity be a disturbing element in bliss, all the more that, unlike similar feelings in this life, it is untouched by hope.[32]

If the argument I have been advancing is correct, it may well be the case that there is nothing incoherent in the idea that perfect human bliss includes a "disturbing element." Of course, the disturbing element could not be predominant and the term may, in fact, be too strong a description. But the blessed may share the moral attitude of regret toward their fellow persons who reject the joy of God's kingdom. In short, the blessed may share God's perspective and consequently share God's perfect happiness, a happiness which could be compatible with some element of suffering.

VI

As I noted in the Introduction, traditional accounts of hell have been rejected primarily because of moral problems. These problems are sharpest when viewed in light of the Christian claim that God is perfectly good. In this chapter, I have argued that the doctrine of eternal hell is compatible with God's perfect goodness. This task might be relatively easy if one assumed that God's goodness is fundamentally different from our ordinary conception of goodness. I have, however, assumed a strong account of divine goodness which I believe accords with our own deepest moral intuitions. In particular, I have affirmed—following Wesley—that

God's goodness entails that he loves all creatures, impartially desires that all of them be happy, and is willing to do whatever he can, short of overriding freedom, to give happiness to all. If my argument is sound, and at least some traditional accounts of hell are compatible with God's goodness as construed in this chapter, then the moral problems we have noted are not beyond resolution.

5

HELL AND HUMAN FREEDOM

So far we have considered the traditional doctrine of hell from the standpoint of the divine nature and found that at least some versions of the doctrine are compatible with perfect knowledge, power, and goodness. Even if God has infallible foreknowledge of all future events, is almighty, and gives all persons an optimal measure of his grace, it is possible, so far as the nature of God is concerned, that some will choose evil decisively and be damned.

Yet difficult questions remain. These have to do primarily with my claim that evil may be chosen decisively. It may be objected that this is not really a credible notion, so the account of hell which I have been developing remains dubious. An account of hell must not only be compatible with the divine nature, it must also be compatible with what we know about the nature of free creatures. And it is such knowledge, particularly our knowledge of human freedom, which makes doubtful the whole notion that anyone could choose evil in the decisive way required for eternal damnation.

It must be emphasized that the kind of freedom assumed by those who take this line is of the libertarian variety. What this points up is that libertarianism poses distinctive problems for the doctrine of eternal hell, just as compatibilism does. As we have already seen, compatibilism raises a particularly severe moral question: how can it be the case that anyone will go to hell if all events, including our "free" choices, are determined by a perfectly good God? Libertarianism involves perplexities of another sort. Here the question is: why would anyone choose to go to hell if he could do otherwise, if it were really "up to him" to decide? The idea that anyone would, of his own accord, make such a choice seems ultimately to be unintelligible.

II

One way of responding to this claim is to point out that such choices have been powerfully and persuasively depicted in great literature. For an example, we could cite Graham Greene's novel *The Heart of the Matter*, which tells the moving tale of a West African police officer named Scobie. He is a man who conducts both his personal and professional life on the highest level of integrity, contrary to the prevailing corruption around him. Despite his honesty and competence, he is passed over for promotion to commissioner.

His wife is very disappointed and becomes increasingly discontented with living in West Africa. In order to make her happy, Scobie decides to send her away on an extended vacation. Since he cannot afford it, he is forced to borrow money from an unscrupulous trader. Other small compromises follow until eventually Scobie's whole character unravels. He becomes involved in a sexual affair and is guilty of complicity in the murder of his servant, of whom he had become unjustly suspicious. Later his wife returns, and his life is further complicated by his efforts to please both her and his mistress. Ultimately, Scobie sees only one way out of the tangles in which he is caught and takes his own life.

Greene's story raises many questions, but for our present concerns one of the scenes late in the book is of particular interest. In this scene, Scobie has gone to see his mistress shortly after going to confession and then to mass. At confession, Scobie had refused to promise the priest that he would stop seeing Helen, his mistress. And the next day, while attending mass without absolution, he decides that he is damned. Then, as he visits with Helen, he tries to tell her how much he has sacrificed to love her. He tells her that he has given up the hope for salvation.

> She said, "If there's one thing I hate its your Catholicism. I suppose it comes of having a pious wife. It's so bogus. If you really believed you wouldn't be here."
>
> "But I do believe and I am here." He said with bewilderment, "I can't explain it, but there it is. My eyes are open. I know what

I'm doing. When Father Rank came down to the rail carrying the sacrament . . ."

Helen exclaimed with scorn and impatience, "You've told me all that before. You are trying to impress me. You don't believe in Hell any more than I do."

He took her wrists and held them furiously. He said, "You can't get out of it that way. I believe, I tell you. I believe that I'm damned for all eternity—unless a miracle happens. . . . "[1]

This episode is interesting because of its portrayal of a character who chooses evil "with his eyes open." Even with the prospect of eternal hell in full view, Scobie chooses to go further into evil, rather than repent. He rejects unequivocally any suggestion that he does not know what he is doing, or believe what he is saying.[2]

A more famous example of a decisive choice of evil is that of Satan in Milton's *Paradise Lost*. At the outset Satan defends his revolt against heaven by proclaiming that it is "Better to reign in Hell, than serve in Heav'n."[3] And later in the drama, he resists thoughts of repentance, and confirms himself in evil.

> So farewell Hope, and with Hope farewell Fear,
> Farewell Remorse: all Good to me is lost;
> Evil be thou my Good; by thee at least
> Divided Empire with Heav'n's King I hold
> By thee, and more than half perhaps will reign;
> As Man erelong, and this new World shall know.[4]

The critic, however, may be unimpressed by such examples. All these show, he may argue, is that a decisive choice of evil is in some loose sense conceivable. But a thing which is conceivable is not necessarily possible. So perhaps these literary examples are good illustrations of human imagination, but strictly speaking, depict the impossible. It is sometimes said that life is bigger than logic; perhaps it is also true that life is "smaller" than literature. If so, it remains to be shown that a decisive choice of evil is an intelligible notion.

The claim that it is not an intelligible notion has been advanced recently by Thomas Talbott. Talbott expresses this view in response to Richard Swinburne, who holds that significant freedom must include the freedom to damn oneself. Otherwise, Swinburne argues, "God would have prevented people from opting for a certain alternative; however hard a man tried to damn himself, God would stop him."[5] Talbott objects to Swinburne's comment as follows.

> We all have some idea of what it means to fall into evil or to choose wrongly on a particular occasion. But what could it possibly mean to say that some sinners are trying as hard as they can to damn themselves? What sort of choice does Swinburne have in mind here? The picture I get is something like this. Though a sinner, Belial, has learned, perhaps through bitter experience, that evil is always destructive, always contrary to his own interest as well as to the interest of others; and though he sees clearly that God is the ultimate source of all happiness and that disobedience can produce only greater and greater misery in his own life as well as in the life of others, Belial *freely* chooses eternal misery (or perhaps eternal oblivion) for himself nonetheless. The question that immediately arises here is: What could possibly qualify as a motive for such a choice? As long as any ignorance, or deception, or bondage to desire remains, it is open to God to transform a sinner without interfering with human freedom; but once all ignorance and deception and bondage to desire is removed, so that a person is truly "free" to choose, there can no longer be any motive for choosing eternal misery for oneself.[6]

This passage suggests two related but distinct issues which shall occupy our attention for most of this chapter. First, there is the question of meaning. What could it possibly mean to choose damnation? I will address this question by suggesting a fuller account than I have previously given of what makes the choice of evil decisive. Then I will turn to the second question which Talbott raises explicitly and pointedly, namely, that of motive. Can any motive make any sense of the claim that evil can be chosen decisively?

If these two questions can be successfully answered, I think this will take us a long way in showing that the idea of choosing damnation is a coherent one. Moreover, I think some such account is necessary to establish this claim. In saying this I am agreeing with Talbott that this issue cannot be settled on empirical grounds. That is to say, we cannot decide this matter by insisting that we know from experience that evil can or cannot be chosen decisively. In

our example about Scobie, the decisive choice of evil seems to be
an empirical claim. "I can't explain it," Scobie says, "but there it
is." Like a scientist responding to evidence which does not fit his
theories, Scobie simply seems to be reporting the facts.

While empirical evidence is certainly relevant, I do not think
it can be properly used as a shortcut through conceptual analysis.
Those who study human evil empirically can only tell us that it
is "likely" that certain persons they have encountered have completely sold out to evil.[7] Such judgments must be made with reserve simply because no human person has perfect knowledge of
his fellow human beings. Greene makes this point at the very end
of his book when Scobie's wife is talking with her priest about her
husband's suicide. She assumes, in line with official theology, that
Scobie must be damned. The priest responds that "The Church
knows all the rules. But it doesn't know what goes on in a single human heart."[8] Furthermore, as Talbott points out, we know
from experience that many persons "sink to the depths just prior
to a dramatic conversion."[9] So we cannot be sure from empirical
observation who is on the brink of damnation and who is on the
brink of conversion.

III

With those considerations before us, let us turn now to develop the idea of a decisive choice of evil. I want to approach this
task by looking at some material from a classic work on the subject,
Kierkegaard's *The Sickness Unto Death*. The historic significance
of this work is neatly summed up in the following comment of
John R. Silber.

> St. Paul consolidated the opposition to Plato's moral optimism in
> asserting the power of men knowingly to do evil; Kierkegaard
> consolidated the opposition to Kant's moral optimism in assert-
> ing the power of men to fulfill their personalities in the despair of
> defiance.[10]

Silber's remark also points up that the question of whether
evil can be chosen decisively is closely related to the more fundamental question of whether it makes sense at all to say anyone can
knowingly choose evil. It is central to Kierkegaard's whole argument that evil can be deliberately chosen, and that this belief is of

crucial importance for Christianity. He insisted that the Christian doctrine of sin stands in stark opposition to the Socratic/Platonic view that sin is a matter of ignorance.

> For if sin is indeed ignorance, then sin properly does not exist, since sin is definitely consciousness. If sin consists in being ignorant of what is right, so that one consequently does what is wrong, sin does not exist.[11]

Sin is for Kierkegaard the theological term for despair, which is the main focus of his attention. It is the "sickness unto death" which he is concerned to diagnose in all of its dimensions. The details of Kierkegaard's sometimes labyrinthine analysis need not detain us, but I do want to emphasize the central idea in his concept of despair. To see this, however, we need to grasp another one of his fundamental premises. I have in mind his notion that God has given to each one of us the task of becoming a self. This is a responsibility we cannot avoid, but it is also a marvelous privilege. As Kierkegaard put it, "To have a self, to be a self, is the greatest concession made to man, but at the same time it is eternity's demand upon him."[12]

The task of becoming a self, however, is something no one can accomplish by himself. Indeed, self is a relational concept, and one can become a self only in relation to God. This relationship requires consciousness or awareness on the individual's part, and Kierkegaard is deeply concerned that this is often lacking.

> Ah, so much is said about human want and misery . . . but only that man's life is wasted who lived on, so deceived by the joys of life or by its sorrows that he never became eternally and decisively conscious of himself as spirit, as self, or (what is the same thing) never became aware and in the deepest sense received an impression of the fact that there is a God, and that he, he himself, his self, exists before this God, which gain of infinity is never attained except through despair.[13]

It is because he exists before God and can become a self only in relation to him that being a self is God's greatest gift to human beings. Kierkegaard never tires of emphasizing how remarkable this is.

And what an infinite reality this self acquires by being before God! A herdsman who (if this were possible) is a self only in the sight of cows is a very low self, and so also is a ruler who is a self in the sight of slaves—for in both cases the scale or measure is lacking.... But what an infinite accent falls upon the self by getting God as a measure![14]

So what it means to become a self is to become decisively conscious that one is an eternal spirit. It is to become aware of God's existence and to allow one's entire life to be shaped by that reality. It is consciously to live in relation to God so that one becomes the sort of self, or person, that God desires.

Now here is where despair comes in. Despair is essentially a failure to be related to God. It is an unwillingness to be the self which God demands, or the will to be a self apart from God. Of course, this is not how we normally conceive of despair, for we typically think of it as a profound kind of hopelessness. However, the despair Kierkegaard identifies is closer to our ordinary conception than appears at first sight. Those persons who never become aware of their existence before God are without hope in a very important sense: they have no hope of the things which can be thought possible only in relation to God.

Kierkegaard insists that despair is a condition common to all persons, whether they know it or not, but only those who know they are in despair can escape it. So while despair itself is a dreadful thing, awareness of it is a great advantage. That is what Kierkegaard means in the quote above when he says the "gain of infinity is never attained except through despair." Despair is eradicated in those who consciously will to be the selves they were meant to be, and are thereby "grounded" in God.[15]

With this background, I want to focus on those parts of Kierkegaard's discussion which can help us understand what it means to choose evil decisively. Of particular interest in this regard is his account of what he terms the "continuation of sin." In this discussion, he wants to establish that there is continuity forming in the life of each person. One kind of continuity is that of living consciously before God in faith. This is the sort of continuity which is established in those who are willing to become selves as God intends. In contrast to this, Kierkegaard wants to emphasize that sin can also be a source of continuity.

Indeed, Kierkegaard believes that those who remain in sin come increasingly to be in its power. It can pervade a life so thoroughly that its presence is scarcely even noticed by the sinner.

> So natural has sin become to him, or sin has so become his second nature, that he finds the daily continuance quite a matter of course, and it is only when by a new sin he acquires as it were new headway that for an instant he is made aware.[16]

Because of his conviction that sin can be a source of continuity, Kierkegaard strongly rejects the suggestion that sin is impotent to give shape to a life. To the contrary, he insists that "sin is within itself a consistency, and in this consistency of evil within itself it possesses a certain power."[17] Kierkegaard elaborates on this point by drawing a fascinating parallel between an evil man and a good man. Just as a good man who wants to maintain his integrity and consistency will resist all thought of evil, so an evil man may protect his consistency by guarding against any impulse toward good. He must, so to speak, ward off all "temptation" to do good.

> That is, he has given up the good in despair, it could not help him anyway, he says, but it might well disturb him, make it impossible for him ever again to acquire the full momentum of consistency, make him weak. Only in the continuation of sin he is himself, only in that does he live and have an impression of himself. What does this mean? It means that the state of being in sin is that which, in the depth to which he has sunk, holds him together, impiously strengthening him by consistency. . . .[18]

Here, I want to suggest, is the factor which makes the choice of evil decisive. It is when the choice of evil has become fully consistent that it is decisive.[19] At this point, evil is present through and through a personality, and there is no place left for good even to get a foothold. It never "bottoms out" so to speak, and thus there is little, if any, prospect for a return to good. Perhaps this is at least part of what is involved in the biblical metaphor of hell as a "bottomless pit."[20]

The nature of this consistency can be further illumined by thinking of it in light of the concept of a person as a hierarchy of ordered desires. According to this picture, persons have not only what are commonly termed first-order desires, but also second-order desires, and perhaps still higher ones. For instance, suppose I want to eat a whole black raspberry pie *a la mode*. However, suppose I am on a diet and I know I should not eat the pie. Because of this, I wish I did not want the pie so much. Philosophically, my predicament could be described by saying I have a first-order desire to eat the pie. But, alas, I also have a second-order desire that I not desire the pie.

Now in this case there is conflict or inconsistency between my first- and second-order desires. I can, however, resolve this in one of two basic ways. First, I can somehow bring my first-order desire into line with my second-order desire. To do this I need to cease wanting to eat the pie. Perhaps I can persuade myself that eating it would be unhealthy for me as well as a needless indulgence. Thinking along these lines, I may reach a point where I no longer desire the pie, which would be in harmony with my desire not to desire the pie. On the other hand, I could also achieve harmony by bringing my second-order desire into line with my first-order desire. To do this, I would have to come to see my desire for the pie as a good thing. Perhaps I could convince myself that eating the pie would actually be good for me because of the nutritional value of raspberries. Again, consistency would result because I would now desire to have the desire to eat the raspberry pie.

In view of this picture of human nature, a person who had chosen evil decisively would be a person who consistently wanted evil at all levels of desire. For a concrete example of how this might occur, let us consider a historical case discussed by Eleonore Stump, namely, that of Goebbels, an infamous Nazi. Stump reports that in one passage in his diary, Goebbels reflects on some footage from a German newsreel which shows the devastation of Poland by the German army. As a supporter of Hitler, he views the destruction of Poland as a good thing. In terms of our discussion, he has first-order desires that Poland be destroyed, and second-order desires which agree with his first-order desires.

However, as he viewed the newsreel, Goebbels apparently felt some measure of compassion for Poland, and his first-order desire for its destruction began to weaken. In response to this, Goebbels informs us that he spoke to himself a word of encouragement: "be hard, my heart, be hard." Stump comments as follows.

This exhortation to himself expresses, in effect, a second-order desire. He wants his heart to be hard; that is, he wants to have a first-order will which assents to the sufferings of the Poles and which is consequently in accord with his second-order desires.[21]

Now this example is particularly interesting in view of Kierkegaard's suggestion that evil persons guard against the "temptation" to good, just as the good guard against evil. It is this sort of action which allows them to maintain the consistency they have achieved, and the strength and power which accompanies consistency. If Goebbels does not resist all tendency to pity the Poles, he may weaken and lose the power which enables him to do his job effectively.

But this raises another important issue. Are those persons whose characters are formed by evil really strong? Are such characters properly described as powerful? Let us go back for a moment to Silber's remark, quoted above. He claimed that Kierkegaard rejected Kant's moral optimism by showing how human beings can "fulfill their personalities in the despair of defiance." The "moral optimism" he has in mind is Kant's view that as one declines in virtue, he also declines in personality. In this view, a wicked person will be a weak person.

In rejecting Kant's view, Silber points to such characters as Hitler, Napoleon, and the industrial tyrants of the nineteenth century. Such men were hardly weak, at least in any ordinary sense of the term. The same could be said for Goebbels, and also for such literary examples as Milton's Satan. Strictly speaking, it may be inaccurate to say such personalities are "fulfilled." This term should perhaps be reserved for those personalities who achieve the purpose which God intended for rational creatures. Nevertheless, it does seem right to say, as Kierkegaard remarks, that the consistency of evil "possesses a certain power." This power is admittedly vastly inferior to the power of good. It is, no doubt, a pale reflection of real power. But through the force of consistency, evil persons can embody a sort of strength and power.

This is not to say, however, that evil persons always possess strength and power. Indeed, perhaps it is more often the case that they do not. The more typical evil person may be more like Scobie than like Hitler or Goebbels. Such persons do not actively choose evil so much as passively give way to it. Richard Swinburne comments on this route to damnation:

> it is a possibility that a man will let himself be so mastered by his desires that he will lose all ability to resist them. It is the extreme case of what we have all too often seen: people increasingly mastered by desires, so that they lose some of their ability to resist them. The less we impose our order on our desires, the more they impose their order on us.
>
> We may describe a man in this situation of having lost his capacity to overrule his desires as having "lost his soul."[22]

This picture of damnation is also prominent in C. S. Lewis's *The Great Divorce.* Lewis sketches a number of contemptible characters who refuse heaven because they prefer to cling to assorted petty sins and desires. These creatures are hollow and unsubstantial. They are fragile and altogether unimpressive.

I want to suggest, however, that these characters are also defined by the consistency of evil. Since they have not imposed any order on their desires, as Swinburne puts it, their desires have imposed their own sort of order on them. Their consistency is found in the fact that they always, as a matter of course, yield to their strongest desire.[23]

Broadly speaking, perhaps we can characterize weak evil persons as those who have allowed their second-order desires to become conformed to their evil first-order desires. They have not, as a matter of principle, chosen evil. They have simply rationalized themselves into it rather than resisted it. By contrast, strong evil persons are those who have managed to bring all their first-order desires into line with their evil second-order desires, which represent a more deliberate, calculated will to do evil.

There is, then, no single type of damned character. The damned may display a certain type of strength, but they may also embody various configurations of weakness. The variety here should not surprise us if for no other reason than that human personality can take many shapes. The only common feature of the damned, again, is the consistency of their evil.

If such consistency does not altogether rule out the possibility of returning to good, it does make intelligible why some persons may never do so. Such persons have closed off every apparent avenue by which good may enter. At every point at which grace could have been accepted, evil was preferred. Where such consistency is achieved, evil gains sufficient potency that the possibility of repentance is all but foreclosed. The persons for whom this is true may be accurately described as thoroughly immune to the grace of God.

IV

Having stated what it means to choose evil decisively, let us turn now to the issue of motive. This is the more basic question, and indeed, the credibility of our foregoing analysis depends upon whether we can deal with it. If we cannot say what could motivate a decisive choice of evil, it might be fairly protested that we have yet to show that such a choice is even a meaningful notion.

It is the apparent lack of an intelligible motive which makes Talbott wonder about the supposed meaning of the claim that some might choose to damn themselves. Elsewhere, Talbott has drawn an important distinction which can be used to make the same point. The distinction is between what an agent has the power to do and what is psychologically possible for him to do. As an illustration, he cites Augustine's view that the redeemed in heaven will no longer even be tempted to disobey God, since they will then clearly see that God is the source of happiness, and sin the cause of misery.

> It will no longer be possible, therefore—no longer psychologically possible, one might say, though *that* notion is by no means clear— it will no longer be possible for the redeemed to disobey God. But why should such clear vision and moral perfection detract from their moral freedom? Will not the redeemed in heaven retain the power (though not the will) to disobey God?[24]

It is important to stress the last sentence of this quote. The fact that the redeemed in heaven retain the power to sin is essential to the claim that they remain morally free. If one has the power to do an act, he remains free in his refraining from doing it even if it is *psychologically impossible* for him to do it, so long as he intentionally does as he does and is not compelled by any outside power to avoid the act.[25]

Interestingly, Talbott's account of why no one could have a motive for choosing damnation is essentially the same as his account of why sin is no longer an option for the redeemed. In both cases, the relevant choice is inconceivable because of a clear awareness that God is the source of happiness, whereas sin leads only to misery. So Talbott's argument that there is no intelligible motive for choosing damnation can be put equally well by saying such a choice is psychologically impossible. And since the choice of damnation is psychologically impossible, the end of universal salvation is "foreordained" according to Talbott.

> The more one freely rebels against God, the more miserable and tormented one becomes; and the more miserable and tormented one becomes, the more incentive one has to repent of one's sin and to give up one's rebellious attitudes.... We may think we can promote our own interest at the expense of others or that our selfish attitudes are compatible with enduring happiness, but we cannot act upon such an illusion, at least not for a long period of time, without shattering it to pieces. So in a sense, all roads have the same destination, the end of reconciliation, but some are longer and windier than others. Because our choice of roads at any given instant is truly free in the libertarian sense, we are genuinely responsible for the choices we make; but because no illusion can endure forever, the end is foreordained.[26]

The challenge, then, for the defender of traditional accounts of hell is to show that there can be motives for choosing damnation, so the choice is in fact psychologically possible. And this challenge is, I think, one of the most difficult to be faced by defenders of the traditional doctrine. Despite the difficulty of the problem, however, I think at least a partial answer can be provided.

For a start, let us reflect on the words which Milton attributes to the fallen Satan: "Better to reign in Hell, than serve in Heav'n." And later, confirming his resolve, he proclaims; "Evil be thou my good." Both of these lines reveal the logic which makes intelligible the decisive choice of evil. Such a choice is possible because hell can somehow be judged better than heaven, just as evil can be seen as a good to be desired.

Of course, objectively speaking, it cannot be better to be in hell on any terms than to be in heaven. And in the same sense, evil cannot truly be good. But if the choice of hell is an intelligible one, there must be something about the subjective experience of choosing evil which can account for why some may prefer it to goodness.

Let us explore this further by considering another example. One of C.S. Lewis's characters is a "Big Ghost" who is shocked to find that one of his former employees, a murderer, is in heaven. The employee has been sent to instruct him and help him so he, too, can remain in heaven. The Big Ghost, however, finds this arrangement insulting. He protests against the unfairness, insisting that all he wants is his rights. He has tried his best, he claims, to be a decent man, and he wants nothing to do with "charity." He does not want to be accepted on the same terms as the murderer. When told that he cannot make it in heaven without help and that his former employee is the one sent to help him, he decides to return to hell.

> "So that's the trick is it?" shouted the Ghost, outwardly bitter, and yet I thought there was a *kind of triumph* in its voice. It had been entreated: it could make a refusal: and this seemed to it *a kind of advantage*. "I thought there'd be some damned nonsense. It's all a clique, all a bloody clique. Tell them I'm not coming, see? I'd rather be damned than go along with you. I came here to get my rights, see? Not to go snivelling along on charity tied onto your apron strings. If they're too fine to have me without you, I'll go home." It was *almost happy* now that it could, *in a sense, threaten*.[27]

This passage conveys the essential insight which makes intelligible the decisive choice of evil. Notice the words I have emphasized. The Big Ghost felt a kind of triumph, and seemed to gain a kind of advantage. Because he was, in a sense, able to threaten, he was almost happy. And it is this, I think, which provides the motivation for the choice of damnation. Those in hell may be almost happy, and this may explain why they insist on staying there. They do not, of course, experience even a shred of genuine happiness. But perhaps they experience a certain perverse sense of satisfaction, a distorted sort of pleasure.

Another way of making this point is by noting that something like happiness may be defined, at a very basic level, as getting what one wants. In view of this, it may be that those in hell approximate happiness in some sense because they get what they want. Lewis's character, for instance, wants to maintain his feeling of superiority over other persons. He wants to hold on to his feeling that he has been treated unfairly. This gives him a feeling of power and indignation which he relishes.

Not surprisingly, a similar character is portrayed for us by Kierkegaard. He is a person who has suffered some form of earthly distress and comes to despair that he will ever be relieved of it. His anger at what he has had to undergo turns into resentment at the whole of existence. He imbibes this so deeply that he reaches a point where he is no longer willing to be relieved of his distress. Indeed, it is now a part of his very identity. He considers himself a proof against the goodness of existence and he must hold out against repentance in order to maintain his protest.

> Even if at this point God in heaven and all his angels were to offer to help him out of it no, now he doesn't want it, now it is too late, he once would have given everything to be rid of this torment but was made to wait, now that's all past, now he would rather rage against everything, he, the one man in the whole of existence who is the most unjustly treated, to whom it is especially important to have his torment at hand, important that no one should take it from him for thus he can convince himself that he is in the right.[28]

The sketch of this character is particularly interesting because it shows how the choice of evil could be sustained indefinitely, even forever. Even if this person is not in bondage to sin in such a way that he *cannot* repent, we can still see how he may never want to. For his resentment seems to perpetuate itself. The longer he holds out, the more he has invested in maintaining his indignant posture. And the more he invests, the more motivation he has to keep it up.

Notice also that this person wants to maintain his torment so "he can convince himself that he is in the right." Ironically, another aspect of the motivation for evil is the desire for vindication. The evil person wants to be right, and he will pay an astounding price in order to maintain his claim to righteousness.

Perhaps this is one of the clues we need to understand Jesus' story of the rich man and Lazarus.[29] Although the rich man is in torment, he does not seem ready to repent. To the contrary, he is more concerned to justify himself. This seems to underlie his request that Abraham send Lazarus to his five brothers to warn them "so they will not also come to this place of torment." Implicit in this request is the suggestion that he himself was not fairly warned about the place of torment. Had he known, he would have lived differently. It is not that he failed to do what he knew was right; he was not properly informed as he should have been. Since he has not been treated fairly, he would at least like his brothers to be.

Of course, there is always a danger of reading too much into the details of the parables which Jesus told. These usually make one central point, and it is a mistake to look for meaning in each detail. But insofar as this parable teaches us anything about the nature of hell, I think it shows the tendency of the damned to justify themselves by holding to their claim of righteousness.[30]

Kierkegaard saw another example of this irony in the person who despairs of the forgiveness of sins. They have sinned so much they think they cannot possibly be forgiven. Kierkegaard comments that "despair over sin is not indisposed to bestow upon itself the appearance of something good. So it is supposed to be an expression of a deep nature which thus takes its sin so much to heart."[31] Thus, the person who goes on in sin because he thinks he cannot be forgiven may actually be engaging in a subtly inverted act of pride. And once again, it is evil assuming a posture of moral superiority and righteousness.

What all these cases show us, I want to emphasize, is that hell may afford its inhabitants a kind of gratification which motivates the choice to go there. In each case the choice of evil is somehow justified or rationalized. In each case there is an echo of Satan's claim that hell is better than heaven. That belief is what finally justifies and makes intelligible the choice of hell.

So conceived, we can say hell is a sort of distorted mirror image of heaven. There is no place in it for the strength of real moral character, but an imitation of this can be had by those who deliberately achieve consistency in evil. It can offer no true righteousness, but it does offer the alternative attraction of self-righteousness. It holds no genuine happiness, but those who prefer it to heaven may savor a deformed sense of satisfaction which faintly resembles real happiness. Hell cannot truly be heaven, or be better than heaven, any more than evil can be good. But this lesson may be finally lost on those who persist in justifying their choice of evil by calling it good.

V

Now at this point, an important question must be raised. What is implied in the idea that those who choose hell rationalize or justify their choice by insisting that hell is better than heaven? Is it not implied that such persons are deceived or mistaken about what is good? And if they are deceived, how can it be said that they have chosen hell consciously and willingly? Is this not a tacit admission that such a choice, despite the above argument, is an impossible one?

In response to this, I want to agree that those who choose evil, and ultimately hell, are indeed deceived. I want to insist, however, that the deception is self-inflicted. Those who prefer hell to heaven have convinced themselves that it is better. In their desire to justify their choice of evil, they have persuaded themselves that whatever satisfaction they experience from evil is superior to the joy which God offers. At the very least, they see some advantage to be gained in the choice of evil.

The last line deserves emphasis, for it leaves open the possibility of real perversity, the possibility that some may choose evil just because it is evil. Such persons would not be deceived in the sense that they think evil is good in some way. Rather, they recognize evil for what it is. However, I would insist that even perverse persons must gain some sort of satisfaction from their choice of evil. They must take some corrupt pleasure in choosing evil because it is evil. Perhaps such a choice represents the epitome of self-assertion and independence from moral norms. Maybe it gives an illusion of complete autonomy that no other sort of choice does.[32] It is admittedly hard to conceive of such a choice, but if real perversity is an option for free persons, it must be possible to see some advantage in choosing evil because it is evil.

But now the question may take another direction. Supposing that some could be self-deceived to the point that they prefer hell, couldn't God remove their deception? Talbott argued, we recall, that it is always open to God to break a sinner's bondage to desire or dispel his deception, without in any way interfering with his freedom. While this claim can seem plausible enough, I doubt whether it is true. It seems to me that the ability to deceive ourselves may be an essential component of moral freedom, at least initially. If we cannot deceive ourselves, there can be no sustained motive to choose evil, and hence no freedom to so choose. If we lack the capacity to maintain indefinitely our self-deception, Talbott is mistaken in his insistence that our choice of roads is always "truly free in the libertarian sense."

But surely, as Talbott has argued, one can have moral freedom without having any motive at all to do evil. The redeemed in heaven enjoy perfect moral freedom but it is psychologically impossible for them to disobey God since they no longer have any motive to disobey, and the love of God has removed any possibility of perversity from their lives. And as we have noted, Talbott thinks the choice of damnation is psychologically impossible for essentially the same reason that the choice of sin is psychologically impossible for the redeemed. In both cases the choice cannot be made in view of the clear knowledge that God is the source of happiness, and sin the cause of misery.

Now this parallel between the two cases is provocative, but it raises some important questions. In the first place, must this knowledge be present in any agent as a prerequisite for his choosing damnation? Talbott apparently thinks so. In his account of Belial, Talbott assumes Belial must have this knowledge if it is meaningfully to be said that he could choose damnation. But again, Talbott's point is that the possession of this knowledge renders such a choice unintelligible.

This brings us to another cluster of questions which take us to the heart of the matter. How is this knowledge acquired? Can it be acquired only through free response to God's grace? Or does God somehow impose it upon us or make it impossible for us to avoid?

Before examining Talbott's view further, I want to sketch my own response to these questions. In my view, the knowledge that God is the source of happiness, whereas sin is the source of misery, is acquired in its full clarity only through free response to God's grace. As one responds to God's grace, in other words, he gains a deeper and deeper understanding of God's relation to happiness. This understanding, I want to emphasize, is not a matter of mere intellectual insight. Rather, it is a matter of moral development and character. And it is because of this character that the saints in heaven spontaneously love God and want to do his will. Those who have responded to God in this fashion and achieved this character can be said to have perfected their moral freedom.

But on the other hand, those who have not achieved this character can resist God's grace. At this stage of moral and spiritual development, knowledge of the connection between God and happiness must be relatively unformed. This knowledge must be fully adequate to encourage pursuit of God and the resulting character growth, but limited enough to allow us to deceive ourselves, resist God's grace, and derail our character development.

This point must be related to my account of optimal grace in the previous chapter. There I suggested that such grace involves being fully informed about Christian faith and teaching. What I want to stress now is that self-deception is compatible with being so informed. Self-deception is not a matter of lacking information, but rather a matter of not attending to what one knows, or of suppressing it and refusing to act on it. So the person who fails to achieve a profound understanding of God's relation to happiness does not do so ultimately because he is uninformed about Christian truth. He has, however, ignored what he knows in this regard and has chosen to live as if it were not true. As I have already argued, one can do this to the point that his character is thoroughly formed by evil. In such a condition, when a person no longer feels any desire to respond to God or do the good, we may say one has thoroughly perverted his moral freedom.

So in the end, one either perfects his moral freedom or he perverts it. In the former case, one has lost all motivation to do evil, whereas in the latter, one has lost all motivation to love God. But initially, I want to stress, moral freedom requires both the ability to respond to God's grace as well as the ability to resist it. And the latter requires the ability to deceive oneself, which entails the ability to avoid clear perception of God's relation to happiness.

By contrast, Talbott apparently thinks clear perception of this truth is finally unavoidable. To see why this is so, let us recall his account of why the end of universal salvation is foreordained. This is the case, Talbott thinks, "because no illusion can endure forever." The particular illusion he has in mind is the notion that our selfish actions and attitudes are compatible with our enduring happiness. This illusion is always shattered in the long run, Talbott insists, because the more one rebels against God, the more miserable and tormented he becomes; and the more miserable and tormented he becomes, the more incentive he has to repent. Finally then, repentance is inevitable for all persons.

Now I am inclined to agree with Talbott that universalism follows if we grant his claim that no illusion can endure forever. But if he is correct in his account of why this is so, then it is apparent that God forces some persons to give up their sinful illusions. For if God causes those persons who continue to rebel against him to grow *ever* more miserable and tormented, then it seems that God is imposing on those persons the clear knowledge that he is the source of happiness, and sin the cause of misery. No one can avoid this knowledge for the simple reason that no finite being can continue endlessly to choose greater and greater misery for himself. So in the end, the knowledge which makes impossible the choice of damnation is not acquired through free choice, but is itself impossible to avoid.

Talbott's account is reminiscent of a procedure employed in England centuries ago to induce persons accused of a felony to plead either Guilty or Not Guilty before the court, so they could be tried by jury. That procedure, according to Alec Kassman, "was to press the accused under iron weights until he either consented to plead or died."[33] My point in making this comparison is to insist that there is a limit on how much "pressure" our freedom can bear. Just as a person who is subjected to ever increasing pressure from weights will at some point die, so will a person's freedom at some point be destroyed if his repentance is induced by ever-increasing torment and misery.

Of course, God is the only one who knows us well enough to know at what point our freedom is broken. Only God knows how much inducement through misery one can stand before his freedom is eliminated. But again, my claim is that there is a limit to what freedom can tolerate, and if a person resists to that point, then God cannot add more pressure without violating his freedom. To be sure, if God added such further pressure, the person would be forced to see that sin causes misery and would find it impossible not to submit to the pressure. But the choice to submit under these circumstances would not qualify as a free choice.

This point can also be made in terms of Talbott's distinction between what is psychologically possible for an agent and what is within his power. I am claiming that the inability to choose greater and greater misery for oneself represents not so much a psychological impossibility as a limitation on our power. It is not, in other words, within our power to endure ever-increasing misery. We do not have the constitutional strength or capacity to absorb ever greater amounts of torment. By contrast, some things are psychological impossibilities for us not because of limitations in our constitutional strength or capacity for endurance, but because of our beliefs or the character we have acquired. The redeemed in heaven find sin impossible not because they lack the constitutional strength necessary to sin, but because their character, shaped by the clear knowledge that God is the source of happiness, will not permit it.

Now to summarize the argument in this section, I have been trying to show that the choice of hell is psychologically possible because we are able to deceive ourselves. We can grant that Talbott is correct in holding that the choice of evil is impossible for anyone who has a *fully formed* awareness that God is the source of happiness and sin the cause of misery. But the crucial issue is whether we are able to avoid this knowledge or whether it is just as impossible to avoid it as it is to sin if we have it. I have argued that on Talbott's view we do not have the power to avoid this knowledge if God forces it upon us by making us ever more miserable as long as we do not repent. If it is not within our power to avoid this knowledge, neither is it within our power to choose damnation. And if this choice is not within our power—as opposed to being psychologically possible for us–then we are not free with respect to it. Hence God cannot always remove our (self-imposed) deception without interfering with our freedom. If God allows us to retain libertarian freedom, some illusions may endure forever.

VI

Let us turn now to consider another of Talbott's claims which we have already noted, namely, his claim that God can always release a sinner from his bondage to desire without interfering with his freedom. Talbott defends this notion as follows:

> Is it not precisely the function of the Holy Spirit, according to Christian theology, to release sinners from their bondage to sin? And if a loving God can do this once, can He not do it again and

again? The argument that a loving God would not interfere with human freedom has no relevance in a context where, *by hypothesis*, we are speaking of those who have already lost their freedom, who are prisoners of bad desires.[34]

Talbott goes on to illustrate with the case of a physician who treats a patient for addiction to heroin by readjusting the balance of chemicals in his brain. The physician is not interfering with the patient's freedom, even if the patient is not able at the time to give his free consent to the treatment. Rather, the physician is restoring the patient's ability to make free choices.

But suppose, however, that the patient had deliberately chosen to become addicted to heroin. Suppose he had, in a decisive way, made the choice to become addicted and had made it clear to his family and friends, before he actually became addicted, that he did not want any medical treatment. In this case, if the physician thwarts the patient's desire to remain an addict by restoring the chemical balance in his brain, it seems he is interfering with his freedom to become the kind of person he wants to become.

Although this example is rather implausible, it does help us get some picture of how a person might make a thorough choice to follow his desires until he could no longer resist them. A person might make such a choice because he did not want to exercise the discipline necessary to impose order on his desires. In this case also, it does not seem that God could "again and again" release such a sinner from bondage without interfering with his freedom. The sinner might resent being faced over and over with the choice either to impose order on his desires, as Swinburne put it, or allow his desires to impose their order on him. He might prefer in a settled way the latter alternative and find it ever more annoying that God will not, once and for all, let him have what he wants.

But couldn't God simply take away his preference to give way to his desires? Couldn't God change him in some way so that he would be willing to bring order to his desires and form a good character?

Surely God could work such a change in a person. The question, however, is whether God could do so without decisively, and even destructively, overriding the person's freedom. Indeed, if God were unilaterally to remove certain basic and morally significant preferences from a person and replace them with other preferences, it is unclear whether this would even be the same person. In other words, questions of personal identity must be faced, given certain conceptions of how God might change a person.

But leaving these aside, couldn't God legitimately override a person's freedom in order to prevent his damnation? As I noted in the previous chapter, Talbott holds that a perfectly good God would do this. In fact, this is his last line of defense against the view that some persons may freely and decisively choose evil.

Talbott defends his view by pointing out that there are cases in which we feel justified in interfering with the freedom of other persons. In the first place, we may be justified in interfering with the freedom of another in order to prevent one person from doing irreparable harm to another. And second, we would also feel justi-fied in interfering with the freedom of another if it was necessary to prevent that person from causing himself irreparable harm. For instance, Talbott points out that a loving father would physically overpower his daughter to keep her from committing suicide.

The second case is particularly relevant to our concerns, so let us focus on it. Talbott is certainly correct, I think, to hold that a father would be justified in interfering with his daughter's freedom to prevent her from taking her own life. I want to suggest, however, that there are important differences between this case, and the choice of damnation, as I have described it. The main difference, I think, is that in the case of suicide, the father can rightly assume that his daughter has in some way temporarily, as we say, "lost her senses." She has become overly distraught by something, or perhaps overwhelmed by depression. Given time to get hold of herself and gain a better perspective, she will be grateful to her father for saving her life.

But on the other hand, this sort of description does not apply to those who choose evil decisively. They would not change given more time or the opportunity to gain a better perspective. Their choice of evil is not a rash, temporary impulse which might later be regretted. Nor can it be assumed that they would be grateful if God interfered and gave them another opportunity to go right.

So the fact that we should interfere with the freedom of oth-ers to prevent them from suddenly doing irreparable harm to them-selves does not clearly provide reason for God to interfere with human freedom to prevent damnation. Indeed, if we had God's perfect understanding of others, we might not always be justified in preventing the choice of others irreparably to harm themselves. If we knew the choice was fully deliberate and would not later be regretted, we could, I suggest, have good reason to respect the person's freedom to make such a choice. But since we do not have such perfect knowledge, we should always assume otherwise and interfere with such choices.

My assumption, however, that a person should ultimately have the right, if he so chooses, to do himself irreparable harm obviously involves a strong commitment to the value of libertarian freedom. This value judgment is surely one of the main pillars of the orthodox Christian doctrine of hell, and indeed, I think the doctrine would topple without it. As I noted in the previous chapter, the judgment that freedom is this valuable may represent a ground-level intuition. As such, it cannot easily be defended without appeal to something equally controversial. It is worth remarking, however, that placing an extremely high value on human freedom is not a Christian idiosyncrasy. To the contrary, worldviews as divergent from orthodox Christianity as those of atheistic existentialism and process philosophy also place an extremely high value on human freedom. So it can at least be said that the Christian who appeals to the value of libertarian freedom to defend his belief in hell is making his case on the basis of a widely shared intuition.

The value of human freedom may provide an answer to another question we have yet to consider: why doesn't God simply annihilate the damned? Or in the same vein, why wouldn't God allow the damned to annihilate themselves, to commit ultimate metaphysical suicide?

The answer may be that this would detract from the seriousness of moral freedom. Such freedom, in its most significant form, requires that we live with the consequences of our choices, at least our decisive choices. Our choices are far more significant if the consequences are eternal and inescapable rather than merely temporal, or, like the choice of annihilation, eternal but escapable because not experiencable.

But, the question may persist, would a perfectly good God require such weighty choices from us? The answer I think is yes, if it is God's will that we choose right, and God gives us every opportunity to so choose. In other words, the fact that God gives us optimal grace justifies his presenting us with such significant choices, for it is optimal grace which makes clear that everyone really gets what he wants.

Now some will find this whole line of argument unsatisfactory and insist that if God is truly merciful, he would either annihilate the damned or allow the damned to annihilate themselves. If God is gracious he would not make people face the consequences of their wrong choices, at least not forever.

At this point, the defender of the doctrine of eternal hell may seem to have little recourse except to point out that the objector is relying on a controversial moral judgment which is far from obvious. There is, however, another line to be taken, namely, to challenge the objector's assumption that the damned would *want* to be annihilated. The objector takes this for granted, but it can be plausibly maintained that the damned may not desire extinction. And if they do not, this strengthens my previous claim that everyone gets what he wants. Some want a loving relationship with God and other persons in heaven, whereas some prefer to cling to their sins in hell, but none finally want total extinction.

The obvious rejoinder here is to point out that some apparently desire extinction for they commit suicide. At first glance, this seems to be a decisive objection to the line I have just proposed. It is not, however, for it does not obviously follow from the fact that some commit suicide in this life that the damned would prefer annihilation over existence in hell. Maybe the distorted pleasures of hell are sufficient from the viewpoint of the damned to make life in hell preferable to extinction. If so, it is an act of mercy for God to allow them to retain their existence.[35]

Perhaps these thoughts can be put in perspective by coming back to Kierkegaard's exclamation: "But what an infinite accent falls upon the self by getting God as a measure!" The notion that a life characterized by some degree of pleasure could be hell may seem implausible initially, but it makes a good deal of sense if we remember that the good according to Christianity is not an ordinary thing. Rather, it is the extraordinary opportunity to live before God, in conscious relationship to him. The choice of evil is fundamentally the preference of something else to this good. It is because the good is so wonderful that something as objectively terrible as hell is possible. Perhaps the choice of hell is intelligible partly because anything chosen in favor of such a relationship to

God could only be hell in comparison. And it is perhaps because the good is so extraordinary that some are able to persuade themselves that they do not prefer it. Or so Kierkegaard thought at any rate, as his following remark suggests.

> It is now high time to explain that the real reason why man is offended at Christianity is because it is too high, because its goal is not man's goal, because it would make of a man something so extraordinary that he is unable to get it into his head.[36]

Whatever one thinks of this argument, I want to emphasize that it represents a second distinct option for responding to the claim that God should annihilate the damned. One can maintain that the seriousness of our moral freedom rules this out, or one can propose reasons for thinking the damned do not want extinction. Either way, one can uphold the traditional view that our final choice is between eternal heaven and eternal hell.[37]

The main thrust of the chapter has been to argue that even when the choice is thus narrowed, some may elect eternal hell. Now, as at the beginning of this chapter, the claim that such a choice is possible strains credibility. I have addressed this perplexity by trying to show that an intelligible account can be given not only of what it means to choose evil decisively, but also of the motivation involved. My case has hinged crucially upon the notion that a person can so deceive himself into believing evil is good, or at least holds sufficient advantage to be gained, that he comes to the point where he consistently and thoroughly prefers evil to good. I will be satisfied if the case I have argued has made even partially comprehensible the remarkable claim that some may likewise come to prefer hell over heaven.

6

HELL AND HUMAN MISERY

I

I have now addressed what I take to be the main difficulties in the traditional doctrine of hell. If my argument to this point is successful, I think it is fair to claim I have shown that at least some versions of the traditional concept of hell are compatible with both human nature and the divine nature. Such versions are neither immoral nor unintelligible.

There are, however, some important remaining questions. While these are not as crucial as those already addressed, they do require attention in any fullblown theory of hell. I have in mind what we might broadly call ontological questions. In particular, what is the nature of the suffering in hell? Is it only psychological and emotional, or does it also include a physical dimension?

These questions naturally arise because hell has traditionally been conceived as a place of great misery. This is true not only in the popular imagination, but in serious theology as well. Even more significant is the fact that this idea of hell is firmly rooted in the Bible, particularly in the teachings of Jesus. Jesus describes hell as a place of fire, and alternately as a place of darkness "where there will be weeping and gnashing of teeth."[1]

Now it might plausibly be objected that the account of hell which I have been developing does not do justice to this aspect of the doctrine. It might be protested that the hell I have described is not a place of misery at all if those who go there actually get what they want and, indeed, prefer hell to heaven.

In response to this, I want to say something more about the nature of hell and why it surely is a place of misery. But this move on my part is likely to draw a different sort of protest. Am I not now on the verge of crossing over into fruitless speculation on a

139

matter which should simply be recognized as a mystery? Indeed, perhaps I have already said more than is warranted by the meager evidence available to us.

This protest also has some merit. It can, however, be easily exaggerated. I am inclined to think that our modern reticence to say anything substantive on such matters as heaven and hell, not to mention other theological topics, is largely a reflection of the fact that we do not take these matters very seriously. It is instructive to compare this attitude toward hell with that of Thomas Aquinas. Aquinas raises numerous questions about hell which most modern readers would surely find quaint at best, if not altogether impertinent. But such questions naturally occurred to Aquinas, and called for an answer, because hell existed for him in the realm of sober ontological reality. Perhaps Aquinas was too confident that he could tell us exactly what hell is like, but he is a healthy check on our own excesses.

In what follows, I will first approach the question of what hell might be like by sketching what some other writers on the subject have suggested, particularly a sample of classical theologians. Later in this chapter I will spell out, in relation to their views, an account of the misery of the damned which accords with the concept of hell I have thus far articulated. I want to spell out my own view in this fashion in order to highlight not only the continuity, but also the contrast, between my view and classical views. It is important to demonstrate sufficient continuity if the account of hell I have defended is to be recognized as an orthodox Christian position. And where there is contrast, it should be motivated by relevant moral or philosophical considerations. In keeping with this concern, I shall conclude this chapter by indicating some of the moral advantages of the view I propose.

II

A good place to begin is with Augustine, whose writings on hell, like his other writings, left a deep and lasting impression on Western theology. Moreover, Augustine gave considerable attention to the nature of the punishment in hell. One of the most fascinating parts of his discussion of this question is his interpretation of Jesus' description of hell as a place where "their worm does not die and the fire is not quenched."[2]

What is at issue for Augustine is how the worm and the fire are to be understood. Some, he observes, have understood both in a spiritual sense. On this interpretation, the fire refers to the anguish of spirit of someone who repents too late, and the worm depicts the grief which consumes his heart. Others have taken a mediating position, understanding the fire as a literal description of bodily punishment, but the worm as a metaphor for spiritual punishment. In response to these options, Augustine wrote:

> for my part, I find it easier to understand both as referring to the body than to suppose that neither does; and I think that Scripture is silent regarding the spiritual pain of the damned, because, though not expressed, it is necessarily understood that in a body thus tormented the soul also is tortured with a fruitless repentance.[3]

As this passage indicates, Augustine is concerned to establish the case that the fire of hell is real material fire and is used by God as a means to punish the wicked in their bodies. By comparison, Augustine plays down the spiritual pain of hell. Indeed, the spiritual pain is conceived here as simply a consequence or accompaniment of bodily pain. It is the torment of "fruitless repentance" in the soul of a person undergoing terrible physical punishment.

Later theologians, however, further developed and emphasized the spiritual dimension of the torment of hell. Aquinas, for instance, interpreted the worm which does not die as "the remorse of conscience."[4] John Wesley also took the worm to be a reference to the guilty conscience the damned will suffer, but he further elaborated on this idea, suggesting that it likewise represents several other distressing feelings and passions. Indeed, Wesley saw significance in the fact that Jesus seems to distinguish between "*their* worm" which does not die and "*the* fire" which is not quenched. Wesley took this to mean that each damned person would bring to hell his own individual "worm" nurtured by his own unique history of sin and evil. The worms of hell, Wesley remarked, "will be infinitely varied according to the various kinds as well as degrees of wickedness."[5] On the other hand, Wesley thought the fire of hell—which he believed to be literal—would be essentially the same for all, except that it might be more intense for some than others, depending on the degree of their guilt.

The fire of hell has also been seen as an image for spiritual misery. Several writers have depicted hell as an internal fire which burns violently in the hearts of the wicked. Dante, for instance, has Virgil speak to one of the blasphemers in hell:

> O Capaneus, by your insolence
> you are made to suffer as much fire inside
> as falls upon you. Only your own rage
> could be fit torment for your sullen pride.[6]

Milton describes Satan's condition the same way. Because of the tumult in his breast, Satan cannot flee hell by a change of place: "Which way I fly is Hell; myself am Hell."[7] And Jonathan Edwards, who is better known for his account of the physical agonies of hell, also gave eloquent expression to the spiritual ruin caused by sin. If God were to leave sin without restraint, nothing more would be needed "to make the soul perfectly miserable." Indeed, "if sin was not restrained, it would immediately turn the soul into a fiery oven, or a furnace of fire and brimstone."[8]

When the misery of hell is construed like this, it is no longer a remote, inconceivable mystery. To the contrary, hell stands in clear continuity with our experience in this world. In other words, we may experience in this world a foretaste of hell. Wesley was quite explicit on this point.

> For it is not possible in the nature of things that a man should be happy who is not holy . . . . The reason is plain: all unholy tempers are uneasy tempers. Not only malice, hatred, envy, jealousy, revenge, create *a present hell in the breast*; but even the softer passions, if not kept within due bounds, give a thousand times more pain than pleasure.[9]

In the same vein, Peter Geach thinks the quality of life in hell is not beyond our understanding. Geach bases his claim on the observation that sometimes, when a person is dying from senility or a terminal illness, he "shows himself as prey to the most violent evil passions: terror, despair, rage, hatred, malice." Up to that point, Geach says, the person has worn a mask. But now he is no longer capable of holding the mask in place, and "the Hell that burns within him becomes visible."[10]

It is important to emphasize that the kind of misery here described is simply the natural consequence of living a life of evil and allowing one's character to be shaped by vicious feelings and emotions. The torment is not imposed externally or arbitrarily. It is just the necessary result of choosing certain kinds of evil.

Now, so far, I have dealt only with the misery of hell which is due to painful or unpleasant feelings. Traditionally, however, it has been emphasized that the punishment of hell is composed not only of such negative feelings or "pains of sense," but also of the loss of what is good. In other words, hell is a matter not only of disagreeable feelings, but also of deprivation. Before turning to consider the physical side of the feelings of hell, let us look at the loss which hell involves.

Of course, the greatest loss of those in hell is that of knowing God and enjoying life with him in heaven. This is the true end for which we were created, and the ultimate tragedy of hell is that some will lose out on the joy of eternal fellowship with God. Moreover, the damned will see what they have lost, and this will add to their torment. According to Aquinas, they will see the blessed before the judgment day and they will be grieved when they see what they have forfeited. After the judgment day, however, they will not be able to see the blessed, but they will remember what they saw before and this will continue to haunt them.[11]

But those who do not recognize God as their measure, as Kierkegaard put it, may not be concerned about this loss. More relevant to their interests is the claim that hell shall be devoid of all the things which make this life pleasant and meaningful. Wesley commented:

> There is no grandeur in the infernal region; there is nothing beautiful in those dark abodes, no light but that of livid flames. And nothing new, but one unvaried scene of horror upon horror. There is no music . . . there is no friendship in hell.[12]

This dimension of the punishment of loss is different from the spiritual misery sketched above in the sense that it is not a direct, natural consequence of being evil.[13] But neither is it, strictly speaking, physical, although this may be involved insofar as hell is pictured as a physically repulsive place.

This brings us to the question of whether hell involves bodily pain. As we have noted, this was already an issue in Augustine's day, and he sided unequivocally with those who held that the fire of hell is literal. Aquinas followed Augustine in this opinion and produced his own extended defense of the view that the fire of hell is corporeal fire, of essentially the same nature as the fire we know. Typical of Aquinas's defense is his response to the often-repeated argument that the fire of hell must not be literal since hell is also described as a place of darkness.

> The disposition of hell will be such as to be adapted to the utmost unhappiness of the damned. Therefore accordingly both light and darkness are there, insofar as they are most conducive to the un-happiness of the damned. . . . Consequently in hell the place must be so disposed for seeing as regards light and darkness that nothing be seen clearly, and that only such things be dimly seen as are able to bring anguish to the heart.[14]

It is also noteworthy that Aquinas held, like Wesley after him, that the fire of hell would torture some persons more than others, according to the measure of their sin. This is possible, Aquinas maintained, because God regulates the fire in keeping with his perfect justice.[15]

Of course, one need not believe the fire of hell is literal in order to believe hell includes some sort of physical pain. John Calvin, for instance, thought the fire of hell is a metaphorical expression, as is the worm. Calvin urged us to

> lay aside the speculations, by which foolish men weary themselves to no purpose, and satisfy ourselves with believing, that these forms of speech denote, in a manner suited to our feeble capacity, a dreadful torment, which no man can comprehend, and no language can express.[16]

As Calvin's remark makes clear, the view that the fire of hell is not literal does not necessarily entail that the pain it signifies is any less intense.

Peter Geach also affirms that hell includes physical pain, al-though he does not believe the fire is literal. Following a sugges-tion of Jonathan Edwards, he proposes that the natural order will function to punish the wicked. At the present time, Geach says, it is a miracle of God's mercy and forbearance that the wicked can employ the inanimate world for their selfish purposes. After the judgment, however, this will no longer be the case:

> when they try to use the inanimate creatures . . . they will find that Nature at last manifestly obeys her Master and not them—and so the ordinary course of Nature will continually frustrate, enrage, and torment them: continually, because their will is obstinate in evil.[17]

There is, moreover, at least one other way of accounting for physical pain in hell which does not require literal fire. Such pain could be inflicted by the animate creatures in hell. In other words, it may be that the inhabitants of hell will inflict pain on one another. Wesley indicated this when he emphasized the kind of company which could be expected in hell. Those who go there, he remarked, are perfectly evil, and there will be no one to restrain them from exerting their wickedness.[18] Likewise, Edwards stated that "other wicked men who shall be there will be like devils; they will have no pity on you, but will hate and curse, and torment you."[19] And in the same vein, Eleonore Stump interprets Dante as presenting a similar account of the physical pain of hell.[20]

By contrast, hell is sometimes conceived as an experience of complete isolation. On this picture, the damned are like prisoners in solitary confinement, whose misery is compounded by the fact that they must bear it utterly alone. C. S. Lewis suggests something like this when he depicts the damned as moving farther and farther away from one another in order to avoid all contact with others.[21] Each damned person is an isolated unit of misery. Each makes up his own individual world of self-inflicted suffering. On the view we just considered, however, there is no escape from the hurt inflicted by others. Hell is a company of persons whose interaction with one another is a source of much of their distress.

These different ways of construing the physical pain of hell are not, of course, mutually exclusive. Edwards, for instance, believed in literal fire, but he also thought punishment would be forthcoming from the world of nature as well as other damned persons. When these factors are combined with the spiritual anguish we have already outlined, what emerges is a conception of hell as a place of the greatest possible misery.

This basic conception of the nature of hell is articulated with explicit clarity by Aquinas. Recall that when he offers an explanation of the composition of light and darkness in hell, his premise is that everything there is "adapted to the utmost misery of the damned." He makes essentially the same point elsewhere when discussing the question of whether the damned will be able to make use of knowledge they acquired in this life. His answer, in brief, is that the damned will have knowledge of things which cause grief, but not of things which cause joy. Again, he is operating on the premise that for the damned, nothing will be lacking that causes sorrow, "so that their unhappiness is consummate."[22]

Aquinas's idea that hell is a place of utmost misery, of consummate unhappiness, neatly summarizes how hell has been conceived by a number of prominent classical theologians. And the horror that even the thought of such a place evokes is compounded by the further claim that hell is eternal. It is this, perhaps, which brings into clearest focus the dreadful nature of hell. Not only does it hold the greatest possible misery for its inhabitants, but there is never any relief from it.

Indeed, the agony of hell is such that, naturally speaking, it could not be borne. But in the life to come, Augustine says, the connection between body and soul "is of such a kind, that as it is dissolved by no lapse of time, so neither is it burst asunder by any pain." If necessary, Augustine says, God can alter the nature of human bodies so they will not be consumed by fire.[23] Similarly, Aquinas says it is due to divine justice that the bodies of the damned will not be consumed in the fire of hell. No matter how great the pain, "it will not sever the body from the soul."[24] Wesley echoes the same thought when he says that regardless of how intense the pain of the damned is, "there is no possibility of their fainting away—no, not for a moment."[25]

Such utter misery is surely beyond our comprehension. But insofar as we can conceive of it at all, it is clear that it would entail a depth of despair and dismay that is beyond anything we can imagine. Edwards developed this thought with remarkable intensity. No one should think, he insisted, that it will be possible to bear up under the punishment of hell. It is altogether vain and foolish for sinners to suppose they will be able to tolerate hell by arming themselves with resolution and firmness of mind.

> However they shall have prepared themselves, and collected their strength; yet as soon as they shall begin to feel that wrath, their

hearts will melt and be as water. . . . They will not be able to keep alive any courage, any strength, any comfort, any hope at all.[26]

This conception of hell could be described paradoxically as unbearable agony and torment which must, nevertheless, be borne. No one can bear up under it, and yet, there is no escape from it or end to it. Moreover, since this conception represents perhaps an unsurpassable notion of misery, it is an appropriate place to end this sketch of traditional depictions of hell. Compressed though it is, this sketch provides sufficient background for me to state my view in relation to some traditional pictures of the doom which awaits the damned.

III

Before turning to this task, I want briefly to consider an important preliminary issue suggested by the previous section. I have in mind the question of whether there is some good reason to think hell must include bodily as well as spiritual pain. Although most traditional theologians have thought the "pain of sense" in hell includes a bodily dimension, this has often been supported in large measure by a literal reading of the biblical imagery about hell. But the element of corporal punishment is not, as we noted in the Introduction, essential to the orthodox view of hell. Moreover, as Edwards remarked, the spiritual anguish produced by sin is all that is needed to make the soul "perfectly miserable." Why, then, is it important to insist that hell must also involve physical suffering?

Aquinas supplied the following argument to answer this question.

> Now, the man who puts his end among created things does not use them as he should, namely, by relating them to his ultimate end. So, he should not only be punished by losing happiness, but also by experiencing some injury from them.

It is apparent that Aquinas has in mind here physical punishment in hell, for he goes on to say that

> this punishment is due to sinners, that from those things in which they set their end they receive affliction and injury. Hence, divine

Scripture not only threatens sinners with exclusion from glory, but also with affliction from other things. For it is said, in Matthew (25:41): "Depart from me ye cursed into everlasting fire, which was prepared for the devil and his angels."[27]

Aquinas's argument is somewhat difficult to assess, for it is not altogether clear what he is claiming. Is he claiming that the sinner somehow mistreats or injures created things by not relating them to his ultimate end, so it is just if they in turn cause him pain? Does the sinner in some way do physical harm to created things when he misuses them, and thereby make it right for them to cause him physical harm in return?

It is hard to see how this could be the case since the primary cause of bodily pain in hell according to Aquinas is fire. It might be suggested, however, that fire acts as a sort of representative of the larger created order. Perhaps God uses it to mete out punishment on behalf of other abused elements of the physical creation.

This suggestion makes at least some sense, but it does not seem helpful as an account of the basis for bodily punishment in hell. For sin is properly against God, not against the created order, at least the inanimate order, of which fire is a representative.

Taking this objection into account, perhaps a more plausible reading of Aquinas's argument is the following. Since the sinner acted against God by means of misusing the physical creation, God should punish the sinner physically by means of the misused physical creation. Read in this way, Aquinas's argument may give support to the account of physical punishment suggested by Geach. That is, it may be fitting that the sinner who chose the created order for his end should experience whatever pain may result when the created order no longer serves the sinner's end, but only the end of glorifying God by obeying his will perfectly.

Construed like this, however, it is hard to see how Aquinas' argument underwrites the intense physical suffering he believed hell to involve. In particular, it is hard to see why the fact that the physical creation will obey God's will instead of the sinner's should entail that the sinner will suffer constant pain from eternal fire. The only way such punishment would be likely to occur would be if God were deliberately to cause all damned persons to experience pain from fire. But in this case the pain would not simply be the natural consequence of the fact that the created order no longer cooperates with the sinner's evil purposes, but instead obeys only God. Indeed, it is not clear why this must involve physical pain at all. For the sinner could experience great frustration because he could no longer use the natural order for his evil purposes, without this involving any sort of physical pain.

So let us turn to consider a second argument intended to show that hell should include bodily pain. This argument is mentioned by Aquinas, although it is not clear that he endorsed it.

> Even as the body cooperates with the soul in merit, so does it cooperate in sin. Now on account of the former cooperation not only the soul but also the body will be rewarded after the resurrection. Therefore in like manner the bodies of the damned will be punished. . . . [28]

The argument here seems to be that the body is something like an accomplice in sin, so it should receive its share of punishment for sin. This is what is suggested by saying the body "cooperates in sin."

It is easy, however, to be misled here by our language. Since the body does not have a will of its own, it is not clear what it means to say it cooperates in sin. It is not as if it does so willingly, or unwillingly, for that matter. Rather, the body simply responds, normally, as the will directs. So, taken at face value, this argument provides little reason to think the body must be punished in hell. And like the previous argument, it fails to provide a rationale for the intense sort of physical suffering which would be caused by everlasting fire.

This discussion could be extended considerably, but this is not necessary for my present purposes.[29] I only want to indicate that the conception of hell as a place including physical punishment has been supported not only by a literal reading of the Bible, but also by philosophical considerations. So there may be good reason to retain belief in bodily suffering even if one has good reason to interpret the language about the fire of hell metaphorically. I will come back to this question in the next section.

IV

Now I am prepared to state my own ideas about the misery hell is likely to hold. To begin, one of my fundamental convictions is that the suffering of hell is the natural consequence of living a life of sin rather than arbitrarily chosen punishment. In other words, the misery of hell is not so much a penalty imposed by God to make the sinner pay for his sin, as it is the necessary outcome of living a sinful life. Peter Geach elaborates on this point.

> God is the only possible source of beauty and joy and knowledge and love: to turn away from God's light is to choose darkness, hatred, and misery. God is not like a jealous parent resenting his children's seeking happiness outside the home; apart from love for God men can find only misery, in this world or in any conceivable world; and God could not make men so that they did not need Him.[30]

Geach's last line deserves emphasis. God could not make rational creatures such as ourselves in such a way that they would not need him for their fulfillment and happiness. Perhaps God could make creatures *similar* to us who would be capable of happiness without him. But if there could be such creatures, the level of happiness they could achieve would be far below what we are capable of. We are created in the very image of God, and as such, we have the capacity to enjoy supreme creaturely happiness through a relationship to him.

Since we have such a nature, it is impossible, in the strictest sense of the word, for us to know our true happiness apart from God. This idea agrees, moreover, with the view of divine goodness I have defended. Since God wants all creatures to be happy, the only way any could end up otherwise would be if their happiness were no longer possible.

This basic account of the misery of the damned accords very much with the traditional emphasis on spiritual and emotional distress as a central component of the suffering of hell. This suffering is seen as the inherent result of cultivating sinful attitudes and feelings. This is reflected clearly in Wesley's observation that "unholy tempers are uneasy tempers." Persons who are energized and motivated by such feelings are naturally and necessarily unhappy.

This needs to be kept firmly in mind when considering the

sort of cases I dealt with in the previous chapter, such as the characters described by Kierkegaard and C. S. Lewis. These persons derive a distorted sense of satisfaction from their feelings of rage, resentment, and self-righteousness. The sense of satisfaction must not, however, be exaggerated. It must be viewed within the context of the fact that such feelings are essentially destructive of true pleasure. They are incompatible with genuine peace, joy, and contentment. A person who is enraged cannot be at peace. One who is resentful cannot be contented. And one who maintains a posture of self-righteousness has a contempt for others, as well as a sense of dishonesty, which clashes with real joy. In short then, I think hell involves spiritual "pains of sense."

Now then, what about physical pains of sense? Is there any good reason to think hell must also include bodily pain as many traditional theologians have insisted? On my view there is. I want to emphasize, however, that I do not agree with the account of physical torment so frightfully depicted by such theologians as Aquinas and Edwards. I do not think the fire of hell is literal, nor do I think hell is an ingeniously contrived place of the greatest possible pain and agony. I do, nevertheless, think hell includes physical distress. My reason for this involves an appeal to the traditional Christian belief that the damned as well as the blessed will be resurrected in their bodies. If the damned will have bodies in hell, it seems only natural to suppose that there will be a bodily dimension to their suffering.

One way to account for physical distress is in terms similar to our construal of the spiritual pain of hell. That is, perhaps it is the natural accompaniment of evil passions and emotions. In our present experience, these certainly have a physical dimension. A person who is bitter and resentful often has bodily pain and discomfort which correspond in some fashion to his uneasy emotions. The whole person, so to speak, shares in the suffering. In view of this, it would not be surprising if the bodies of the damned share in the unpleasant sensations which are intrinsic to evil passions and emotions.

This way of understanding the physical pains of hell could perhaps be supported by a modification of the argument that the body will share in the punishment of sin because it cooperated with the soul in sin. I am suggesting something similar, but significantly different. It is not that the body cooperates in sin. Rather, the point is that since we are embodied persons, there is a bodily aspect to who we are, what we become, and what we experience. So if we become evil persons, energized by unhappy emotions, our bodies will be involved in the pain and suffering we undergo. If there is a fire in the breast which torments the soul, it will disturb the body as well.

I do not, however, think this is the only likely source of bodily suffering for the damned. It may well be that the damned will inflict physical pain on one another, as several traditional theologians have suggested. Those whose characters have been shaped by violence may continue to feed on violence in hell. Again, it is simply the natural consequence of violence to engender further violence.

This is not to say that all the damned will suffer in this fashion. Perhaps those who have been given to a quiet contempt for others will experience as the consequence of their sin isolation from others. Just as heaven has many rooms,[31] so perhaps does hell. All have not sinned in the same manner, so all will not suffer in the same manner. Those theologians have been quite right, I think, who have emphasized that each damned person will suffer in the way appropriate to his sin and the character he has formed.

Now if hell has many rooms, does this mean hell is a place? The answer to this question also hinges, I think, on the claim that the damned will be resurrected in their bodies. If the damned have bodies, it is hard to make sense of hell as anything other than a place. It is, to be sure, also a state. It is a state of spiritual, emotional, and mental misery. These two claims are not, however, incompatible, but rather complementary.

Of course, we must readily acknowledge that we have only a very limited understanding of resurrected bodies. The only such body we have a record of is that of Jesus, and the Gospels make it clear that his resurrected body is quite different in some respects from our mortal bodies. So perhaps heaven and hell are places similarly different from the kinds of places with which we are familiar.

This is not to suggest, however, that hell is a place only in some ethereal sense anymore than it is to suggest that Jesus is only a ghost or a spirit. Jesus' body is a real body which can be touched and handled. Likewise, hell is a real place. Indeed, the very fact that the redeemed are supposed to be in the presence of God in their bodies, whereas the damned are not, seems to entail that heaven and hell are distinct places. I am inclined to think it would be *closer* to the truth to say hell is on some faraway planet than to deny that it is a place.

Now then, what about the pain of loss? Does this also comport well with the conception of hell which I have defended? Of course, the damned lose out forever on the ultimate joy of knowing God, but will hell also be devoid of such things as beauty, music, and friendship, as Wesley held?

With respect to friendship, the answer is not altogether clear. On the one hand, it is hard to see how it could exist in hell since friendship requires love in some degree, and love is excluded where evil completely predominates. Certainly friendship which is deep and lasting could not thrive in hell. But on the other hand, it is conceivable that hell could include some forms of social interaction which resemble friendship to some extent.

Things like music and beauty are likewise difficult to assess. Must these be entirely absent from hell, since God is the source of all beauty? It would seem so. But on the hand, if Nero could fiddle while Rome burned—whether or not he actually did—perhaps the damned can also fiddle. Surely, however, they could not derive any real joy from their fiddling, anymore than someone as tormented as Nero could truly enjoy aesthetic pleasures.

V

It will be clear by now that the picture of hell I have presented is in essential continuity with traditional theology in holding that hell is a place of misery. It is not, admittedly, as gruesome an account of hell as that held by some notable classical theologians. If it were, I could not plausibly hold that some persons may freely choose it. So there are also points of contrast with some traditional ideas. I do not, however, think there is any less reason for a person who desires his ultimate well-being to want to avoid hell if it is anything like I have suggested. Indeed, such a person may have more reason to take hell seriously if the misery it holds is of the kind I have described.

This is the case, I think, because the conception of hell I have defended has a moral seriousness about it that is sometimes obscured or distorted in more frightful accounts. The idea that the misery of hell is the intrinsic consequence of choosing to become a certain kind of person has a stark realism about it that is often absent when hell is depicted as the supreme torture chamber. It is a dreadful but credible thought that we might come fully to prefer the deformed sense of satisfaction endemic to sin, and that God will finally give us what we want.

By contrast, sensational accounts of hell may actually have the effect of trivializing the doctrine or making it seem like an empty threat. Perhaps we can see a hint of this in Jonathan Edwards. Although his sermons on hell sometimes had spectacular results, one nevertheless wonders whether in the long run his frightful depictions of damnation may have helped to undermine serious belief in the idea. Consider the following, which comes at the end of one such sermon.

> I suppose some of you have heard all that I have said with ease and quietness: it appears to you as great sounding words, but doth not reach your hearts. You have heard such things many times: You have been too much used to the roaring of heaven's cannon, to be frighted at it. It will therefore probably be in vain for me to say any thing further to you; I will only put you in mind that ere long God will deal with you . . . . You who now hear of hell and the wrath of the great God, and sit here so easy and quiet, and go away so careless; by and by will shake, and tremble, and cry out, and shriek, and gnash your teeth, and will be thoroughly convinced of the vast weight and importance of these things which you now despise.[32]

It is clear, of course, that Edwards himself is deadly serious about what he is saying. But he also seems to suspect that his congregation is not. So he tries to instill seriousness with ever more severe threats of how fearful God's wrath will be. I am suggesting, however, that Edward's approach was counterproductive. His depiction of hell, terrible though it is, does not give a persuasive account of the moral connection between sin and the unspeakable torment he describes.

If the natural connection between sin and misery is kept at the forefront when discussing hell, there is a further advantage to be gained. By doing so, one can mitigate the Kantian-styled objection that the doctrine of hell has a negative effect on genuine moral motivation. If one is moral only to avoid hell, the objection goes, one is not really moral.

This sort of objection has the most force when the misery of hell is conceived as externally imposed punishment, with no necessary relation to the nature of the sin involved. It loses some of its force, however, when the anguish of hell is seen as an internal component of a life of sin and evil. To choose evil is to choose misery, and the one who so chooses does so freely. On the other hand, the one who resists evil will as a matter of course also be choosing to avoid hell. That is why Wesley could urge us to

> Abhor sin far more than death or hell; abhor sin itself far more than the punishment of it. Beware of the bondage of pride, of desire, of anger; of every evil temper or work.[33]

The one who is duly wary of sin and its bondage needs no further fear of hell to give him reason to be moral.

This will not, however, entirely dispose of the objection, for the Kantian can now rephrase it as follows: If you avoid sin because a natural consequence of it is anguish for you, then you are still selfishly motivated. In that case you do not do your duty for its own sake, so you lack the proper moral motivation. Even if you do the right act, you do not do it for the right reason.

At this point, I am willing to concede to the Kantian that the traditional doctrine of hell does appeal to our self-interest as a reason to love God and be moral. But I want to insist that not all self-interest is selfish, and that proper self-interest is a legitimate part of genuine moral motivation. So the traditional doctrine of hell adds positive moral import to the Christian conviction that it is impossible to further one's ultimate best interest by doing what is wrong, just as it is impossible to act against one's ultimate best interest by loving God and doing right.[34]

CONCLUSION

At the outset of this essay, I confronted the controversial nature of the traditional doctrine of hell, particularly the claim that it is morally repugnant. This creates, I noted, a dilemma for the Christian believer. On the one hand, the person who believes in Christ and accepts the authority of his teaching seems inextricably committed to believing the doctrine of eternal hell. If he does not believe this, he undercuts the ground which makes it possible to be a Christian. But on the other hand, if one accepts the doctrine, he seems to be committed to a morally offensive notion.

I believe Christians must squarely face this dilemma. If the doctrine is indeed morally bankrupt or unintelligible, it should frankly and forthrightly be discarded. But if it is not, it should be reclaimed and faithfully taught. Either way, it involves claims of such immense importance that it cannot responsibly be ignored.

I have attacked the dilemma by challenging the purported immorality of the doctrine. I have argued that at least some traditional conceptions of hell are compatible with a very robust account of God's perfect goodness, as well as intelligible from the standpoint of human freedom. Moreover, I have suggested that the doctrine has positive moral value. It underwrites in a way which perhaps nothing else can the claim that we are accountable for our actions and cannot escape responsibility for them. And by portraying how evil can be chosen decisively, this doctrine stands as a stark challenge to any form of moral optimism which denies the reality of radical evil. If the line of my argument is sound, I have shown that Christians can truly believe the doctrine of eternal hell with ethical and intellectual integrity. Indeed, I would suggest that a refurbished version of the doctrine may again play a role in the moral pedagogy of our society.[1]

Those believers who are not convinced by the sort of case I have made, who still find the doctrine of eternal hell either morally repulsive or unintelligible, must take the other horn of the dilemma. That is, they must show that a Christian need not believe the traditional doctrine of hell. This would require somehow

coming to terms with those passages of scripture which have traditionally been read as supporting the idea of eternal hell. Of course,
those theologians who do not consider scripture the primary authority for their theology will be little troubled by this problem.
But among those theologians who feel bound by the authority of
scripture, current trends indicate that more and more are likely to
meet this challenge by interpreting the relevant passages in a way
which accords with either universalism or annihilationism.[2] This is
surely a viable option, if for no other reason than that universalism
has a long tradition which goes all the way back to some of the
Church Fathers.[3]

I would maintain, however, that the burden of proof clearly
rests on those who take this option. The fact remains that the
doctrine of eternal hell has in its favor an impressive consensus
which outweighs the universalist strand in theology. In view of
this, the traditional doctrine of hell should not be abandoned unless the case against it is clear and compelling, both scripturally
and philosophically.

Ideally, it may be thought the scriptural debate on this issue
should be carried out strictly on its own terms, with no consideration of the philosophical case for or against the doctrine of
eternal hell. In reality, however, scripture is seldom, if ever, interpreted in a theological or philosophical vacuum. Nor should
it be. Scripture is properly interpreted in interplay with what is
known from other sources, such as reason and experience. So the
sort of arguments mustered in this essay will be highly relevant
when interpreting those difficult passages of scripture which deal
with hell.

Indeed, given the traditional consensus against universalist
exegesis of scripture, it would be highly implausible to claim that
the case for universalism could be made on the basis of scripture
alone. For this claim to be persuasive, it would have to be shown
that universalism is taught clearly in scripture. But if it is clearly
taught, the traditional consensus against it is extremely odd, to say
the least. The question is inevitable: why have so many Fathers
of the Church down through the ages completely misinterpreted
what scripture plainly teaches at this point? It is apparent, then,
that universalist exegesis can only be convincing when backed
up by arguments that the doctrine of eternal hell is unacceptable

on philosophical or moral grounds. If there are such sound arguments, there is good reason to abandon traditional exegesis at
this point. So in the end, universalist interpretation of scripture
depends heavily on the philosophical case against the traditional
doctrine of hell.

I have tried to show that that case is yet to be made.

NOTES

Introduction

1. The sermon has been anthologized in such volumes as *The American Tradition in Literature*, ed. Sculley Bradley et al. (New York: Grosset & Dunlap, 1974). The following quote is from page 61 of the fourth edition of that book.

2. An editorial description of Edwards's sermon, in the volume just cited, page 55.

3. Jonathan Edwards, *A Narrative of Surprising Conversions* (Wilmington, Del: Sovereign Grace publishers, 1972), 34. The "false hope" is, of course, the false hope of salvation.

4. James Breig, "Hell: Still a Burning Question?" *U.S. Catholic* (Nov. 1977): 7.

5. Ibid., 10, 7.

6. Bertrand Russell, *Why I Am Not a Christian* (New York: Simon & Schuster, 1957), 5.

7. Ibid., 195.

8. Richard J. Bauckham, "Universalism: A Historical Survey," *Themelios* 4 (1979): 48.

9. "The IEA/Roper Center Theology Faculty Survey," *This World* 2 (1982): 50.

10. "Hell's Sober Comeback," *U.S. News and World Report* (March 25, 1991): 56. The poll indicates that 66 percent of Protestants and 57 percent of Catholics believe in hell (p. 57). This represents a considerably different picture of Catholic belief in hell than the figures cited in note 5, above. It should also be emphasized that these figures apply to the general public, unlike the figures in the previous note, which apply specifically to theologians.

11. Ernest Campbell Mossner, *The Life of David Hume*, 2 ed. (Oxford: Clarendon, 1980), 570.

12. J. E. Barnhart, "Theodicy and the Free Will Defense: A Response to Plantinga and Flew," *Religious Studies* 13 (1977): 445.

13. *The Existence and Nature of God*, ed. Alfred J. Freddoso (Notre Dame, Ind.: University of Notre Dame Press, 1983), 3.

14. Robert Short, *Something to Believe In* (San Francisco: Harper & Row, 1978), 34.

15. *Autobiography of John Stuart Mill* (New York: Columbia University Press, 1924), 29.

16. John Stuart Mill, *Three Essays on Religion* (London: Longmans, Green, 1923), 114.

17. Russell, *Why I Am Not A Christian*, 17.

18. Peter T. Geach, *Providence and Evil* (Cambridge: Cambridge University Press, 1977), 123-124.

19. Martin E. Marty, "Hell Disappeared. No One Noticed. A Civic Argument," *Harvard Theological Review* 78 (1985): 391.

20. Ibid., 393. Cf. Gordon Kaufman's remark: "It seems to me we've gone through irreversible changes. I don't think there can be any future for heaven and hell" *Newsweek* (March 27, 1989): 54.

21. Marty, "Hell Disappeared," 394.

22. When Geach's position is spelled out more fully, the dilemma is not as stark as I have put it. For Geach rejects the absolute view of divine foreknowledge assumed in the critique of Mill. He also allows that hell might possibly involve annihilation rather than eternal punishment. But as I have indicated, my purpose here is to lay out the dilemma in its most difficult form.

23. It is worth noting that Marty has doubts about the revival of real belief in hell. He states: "If people really believed in hell they wouldn't be watching basketball or even the TV preachers. They'd be out rescuing people." See "Hell's Sober Comeback," 56. I shall deal with this sort of objection in chapter one.

24. F. W. Farrar, *Eternal Hope* (New York: E. P. Dutton, 1878), xxii-xxiii.

25. Ibid., xxiii-xxiv.

26. E. B. Pusey, *What Is of Faith as to Everlasting Punishment?* (Oxford: James Parker, 1881), 19.

27. Ibid., 10.

28. Ibid., 16.

29. Ibid., 23.

30. See 1 Corinthians 15:20-28; Acts 3:21; Romans 14:9.

31. Farrar, *Eternal Hope*, xvi.

32. John Hick, *Evil and the God of Love*, rev. ed. (San Francisco: Harper & Row, 1977), 345. Hick may, however, be more properly classified as a convinced universalist.

33. Thomas Talbott, "The Doctrine of Everlasting Punishment," *Faith and Philosophy* 7 (1990): 19-42.

1: Hell and Human Belief

1. Charles S. Duthie, "Ultimate Triumph," *Scottish Journal of Theology* 14 (1961): 156-157.

2. The three preceding quotes are all from "Ultimate Triumph," 157.

3. On this distinction, see Alvin Plantinga, "Reason and Belief in God" in *Faith and Rationality*, ed. Alvin Plantinga and Nicholas Wolterstoff (Notre Dame, Ind.: University of Notre Dame Press, 1983), 37.

4. Cf. C. S. Lewis who admitted that he detested the doctrine of eternal hell from the bottom of his heart but nonetheless argued that it has the full support of scripture, tradition, and reason. See *The Problem of Pain* (New York: Macmillan, 1952), 118-119.

5. Bauckham, "Universalism: A Historical Survey," 51. Cited as examples of those who held this view are Tertullian, Cyprian, Augustine, Peter Lombard, Aquinas, and Robert Bellarmine. For a modern defense of the view that pity for the damned is excluded, see Geach, *Providence and Evil*, 138-139.

6. Duthie, "Ultimate Triumph," 170. Note that Duthie refers here to the "Christian consciousness" rather than the Christian heart. He also refers elsewhere to the "Christian mind." All of these terms appear to be used interchangeably.

7. Hendrikus Berkhof, *Well Founded Hope* (Richmond, Va.: John Knox Press, 1969), 62.

8. Søren Kierkegaard, *The Sickness Unto Death*, trans. Walter Lowrie (Princeton, N.J.: Princeton University Press, 1941), 216.

9. Ibid., 221.

10. J. E. Barnhart, *Religion and the Challenge of Philosophy* (Totowa, N.J.: Littlefield, Adams, 1975), 126-127. As a specific instance of this hypothesis, John Hick notes that: "It has been suggested that the theology implied by the title of Jonathan Edwards' famous sermon, 'Sinners in the Hands of An Angry God', reflects God in the hands of angry sinners!" *Evil and the God of Love*, 93n. 1.

11. Ludwig Feuerbach, *The Essence of Christianity*, trans. George Eliot (New York: Harper & Row, 1957), 140.

12. Nicolas Berdyaev, *The Destiny of Man* (London: Geoffrey Bles, 1948), 275-276.

13. Alan Bernstein, "Thinking About Hell," *Wilson Quarterly* (Summer 1986): 84.

14. Richard B. Miller, "The Reference of 'God'," *Faith and Philosophy* 3 (1986): 3-15. As his title indicates, Miller is concerned with the recent debate about reference in philosophy of language. In particular, he argues that the causal theory of reference requires that historical data be taken with metaphysical seriousness. I have not cast my discussion

in terms of the debate about reference, but I accept Miller's point that historical data may be relevant in assessing metaphysical truth claims in religion. My next few paragraphs are largely inspired by Miller's paper.

15. I borrowed this image of the anchor from Miller, page 7.

16. It might be inferred from this that Jesus' experience of temptation was meaningless. For argument to the contrary, see Thomas V. Morris, *The Logic of God Incarnate* (Ithaca, N.Y.: Cornell University Press, 1986), 137-162.

17. Geach, *Providence and Evil*, 135.

18. Peter L. Berger, *A Rumor of Angels* (Garden City, N.Y.: Anchor Books, 1969), 53.

19. Ibid., 65.

20. Ibid., 67-69.

2: Hell and Divine Knowledge

1. *Autobiography of John Stuart Mill*, 29.

2. Apparently, then, to establish a connection between foreknowledge and intention, one must assume some principle like the following: If an agent performs some action A foreseeing that it will have some effect E, and if the agent could prevent E while still performing A, but does not, then the agent intends E. But this alone will not be enough to underwrite Mill's claim. It must also be assumed that God could prevent the effect that some are damned.

3. *Westminster Confession*, II. 2.

4. *Westminster Confession*, III. 2-3, 5.

5. For some suggestions on how Calvinism might be defended, see Thomas P. Flint, "Two Accounts of Providence," in *Divine and Human Action*, ed. Thomas V. Morris (Ithaca, N.Y.: Cornell University Press, 1988), 169-170. The "Calvinism" Flint discusses is that of Thomas Aquinas and his followers. As Flint notes, it is a matter of debate whether Aquinas held strong predestinarian views. It is also worth noting that there are significant areas of agreement between Calvinism and Molinism. See Flint, "Two Accounts," 150-156.

6. *Liberi arbitrii cum gratiae donis, divina praescientia, providentia, praedestinatione et reprobatione concordia* [Hereafter *Concordia*], trans. Alfred J. Freddoso (Ithaca, N.Y.: Cornell University Press, 1988), qu. 14, art. 13, disp. 52, no. 9.

7. The "circumstances" should be thought to include, broadly speaking, the history of the world up to the given time. Features of this history will, of course, have a bearing on the choices of free persons.

8. For a fascinating discussion of this point, see *Concordia*, qu. 14, art. 13, disp. 53, part 2, no. 15.

9. *Concordia*, qu. 14, art. 13, disp. 53, part 3, nos. 13-18.

10. The scripture passages cited by Molina are the following: 1 Samuel 23:10-12; Wisdom 4:11; Matthew 11:20-24.

11. *Concordia*, qu. 14, art. 13, disp. 51, no. 18. See also disp. 52, no. 29.

12. See *Alvin Plantinga*, Profiles, vol. 5, ed. James E. Tomberlin and Peter van Inwagen (Dordrecht: D. Reidel, 1985), 48-52 and 372-382. Plantinga was not, however, aware of Molina's work when he first formulated his free will defense. He reports that when he was first described as a Molinist, he "wasn't sure whether that was commendation or condemnation." (p. 50).

13. *Alvin Plantinga*, 379.

14. Alfred Freddoso concedes that the "account of how God has middle knowledge is arguably the weakest link in the Molinist chain." Introduction to *Concordia*, 52-53.

15. Robert M. Adams, "Plantinga on the Problem of Evil," *Alvin Plantinga*, 232. Adams gives other objections to middle knowledge besides the one I have cited. See also his paper "Middle Knowledge and the Problem of Evil," *American Philosophical Quarterly* 14 (1977): 109-117. Plantinga responds to both papers in *Alvin Plantinga*, 371-382. See also Freddoso's replies to objections against Molinism in his Introduction to *Concordia*, 62-81.

16. Adams, "Middle Knowledge and the Problem of Evil," 110.

17. See 1 Samuel 23.

18. Adams, "Middle Knowledge and the Problem of Evil," 111.

19. Richard Otte, "A Defense of Middle Knowledge," *International Journal for Philosophy of Religion*, 21 (1987): 167.

20. Anthony Kenny, *The God of the Philosophers* (Oxford: Clarendon, 1979), 52-53. See Aristotle, *De Interpretatione*, 9. As Kenny notes, de Rivo's views were condemned by Pope Sixtus IV.

21. Geach, *Providence and Evil*, 52-53.

22. Ibid., 57.

23. Ibid., 58.

24. Kenny, *The God of the Philosophers*, 59.

25. This view should be distinguished from the idea that certain future things may now be said to be true because they are *determined* in their causes, namely, laws of nature and prior states of the universe.

26. Cf. Geach, *Providence and Evil*, 50-52.

27. Richard Swinburne, *The Coherence of Theism* (Oxford: Clarendon, 1977), 175.

28. Richard E. Creel, *Divine Impassibility* (Cambridge: Cambridge University Press, 1986), 98-99.

29. Ibid., 21.

30. Thomas V. Morris, "Properties, Modalities, and God" in *Anselmian Explorations* (Notre Dame, Ind.: University of Notre Dame Press, 1987), 89. It is perhaps worth noting that this view assumes counterfactuals of divine freedom are true (since they are known by God).

31. Swinburne, *The Coherence of Theism*, 176.

32. For Creel's account of creation, see *Divine Impassibility*, 64-79. Creel rejects as incoherent the traditional idea of creation *ex nihilo*, maintaining instead that God created out of what he calls the plenum, which he defines as "the repository of all possibilities not inherent to God" (p. 68). This would have to be taken into account in a full statement of Creel's position but I do not think it is necessary for my purposes.

33. Adams, "Middle Knowledge and the Problem of Evil", 117. Cf. *Alvin Plantinga*, 248-252.

34. Of course, the general foreknowledge view can appeal to the principle of double effect, but this is an option it shares with certain versions of the specific foreknowledge view.

35. Pusey, *What Is of Faith As to Everlasting Punishment?*, 47-48.

36. I have argued elsewhere along this line for taking the historic creeds as normative interpretation of scripture. See *The Problem of Pluralism: Recovering United Methodist Identity*, rev. ed. (Wilmore, Ky.: Bristol Books, 1988), 87-98.

37. It is worth noting, however, that the Athanasian Creed asserts that those who have done evil shall go "into everlasting fire."

3: Hell and Divine Power

1. Geach, *Providence and Evil*, 3-28.

2. For an elaborate defense of omnipotence, see Thomas P. Flint and Alfred J. Freddoso, "Maximal Power," in *The Concept of God*, ed. Thomas V. Morris (Oxford: Oxford University Press, 1987), 134-167.

3. I have in mind particularly the writings of Augustine, Aquinas, and Edwards, some of which I will cite in the last chapter. A reminder is appropriate at this time that I am using the term "Calvinism" generically to denote this broad tradition in theology.

4. *Westminster Confession*, 3.1.

5. *Westminster Confession*, 3.3. In fairness it should be pointed out that many persons in the Calvinist, or Reformed tradition, no longer accept the account of predestination expounded in the *Westminster Confession*. My concern here, however, is not with recent modifications

of Calvinism, but with traditional Calvinism, a relatively familiar and identifiable position which is still influential in a number of Christian circles.

6. *Westminster Confession*, 10.1-2; 4. My emphasis.

7. John Wesley, *Works* (Nashville, Tenn.: Abingdon, 1986), 3:555.

8. *Westminster Confession*, 9.4.

9. *Westminster Confession*, 14.1.

10. John Calvin, *Institutes of the Christian Religion*, ed. John T. McNeil, trans. Ford Lewis Battles (Philadelphia: Westminster Press, 1961), 3.24.8. See also 3.2.11. Special calling, of course, is another term for effectual calling.

11. *Institutes*, 2.3.10.

12. *Institutes*, 3.23.1. The image of God turning wolves into sheep is Calvin's.

13. Flint, "Two Accounts of Providence," 174.

14. See Peter van Inwagen, *An Essay on Free Will* (Oxford. Clarendon, 1983), 114-126.

15. Antony Flew, "Divine Omnipotence and Human Freedom," in *New Essays in Philosophical Theology*, ed. Antony Flew and Alasdair MacIntyre (New York: Macmillan, 1955), 161-162.

16. It should not be inferred from this discussion that there are no significant differences between theological determinism and the physical determinism embraced by many atheistic philosophers. For an insightful discussion of similarities and differences, see Flint, "Two Accounts of Providence," 172-175.

17. It might be argued that it would be more appropriate in this case to say the person does violence to her own will. I could grant this, I think, without having to retract the main point of my argument. For it remains true that God is responsible for making her will in such a way that her choice is contrary to her own will.

18. *Westminster Confession*, 3.7. It should be noted that Calvinists sometimes emphasize that God does not predestine persons to damnation as directly as he does to salvation. Predestination to damnation is more indirect in that God chooses to "pass by" the non-elect, as this passage puts it. That is to say, God chooses to leave them in sin, a condition into which they were born and from which they cannot escape apart from grace. But this does little to alleviate the moral problem, particularly if it is held that God determined the fall into sin. Not surprisingly, Calvinists sometimes suggest that Adam was free in the libertarian sense. I have argued elsewhere that Calvinists cannot consistently do this. See "The Free Will Defense, Calvinism, Wesley, and the Goodness of God," *Christian Scholar's Review* 13 (1983): 22-24.

19. At this point, the Calvinist may object that whatever God does is just and right, simply by virtue of the fact that God wills it. It would

take us far afield to give an adequate response to this objection here. However, I have addressed this issue elsewhere. See my paper "Divine Commands, Predestination, and Moral Intuition," in *The Grace of God, The Will of Man*, ed. Clark H. Pinnock (Grand Rapids, Mich.: Zondervan, 1989), 261–276. See also Philip L. Quinn, *Divine Commands and Moral Requirements* (Oxford: Clarendon, 1978), 156–164.

20. Even if I am wrong about this, and compatibilists can give a satisfactory account of how a person can do other than he is determined to do, my case against Calvinism is affected very little. It remains true on Calvinistic premises that God could save all persons with their freedom intact, but has chosen not to do so. The heart of my objection to Calvinism is that such a view is incompatible with the belief that God is perfectly good.

21. Hick, *Evil and the God of Love*, 342.

22. J. L. Mackie, "Evil and Omnipotence," in *Readings in the Philosophy of Religion*, ed. Baruch A. Brody (Englewood Cliffs, N.J.: Prentice-Hall, 1974), 158.

23. Hick, *Evil and the God of Love*, 275. Hick's "genuine" freedom is, of course, of the libertarian variety.

24. Mackie, "Evil and Omnipotence," 164–165.

25. Strictly speaking, it is more accurate to say God actualizes possible worlds rather than creates them, since they are necessary beings. It can be argued, however, that even possible worlds are objects of God's creation. See Thomas V. Morris and Christopher Menzel, "Absolute Creation," in *Anselmian Explorations*, ed. Thomas V. Morris (Notre Dame, Ind.: University of Notre Dame Press, 1987), 161–178.

26. Thomas P. Flint, "The Problem of Divine Freedom," *American Philosophical Quarterly* 20 (1983): 257.

27. For Plantinga's detailed discussion of these points, see *God, Freedom, and Evil* (Grand Rapids, Mich.: Eerdmans, 1977), 29–55. A more technical and rigorous account appears in Plantinga's *The Nature of Necessity* (Oxford: Clarendon, 1974), 164–190.

28. Hick, *Evil and the God of Love*, 343.

29. Ibid., 276. Hick cites Charles Hartshorne and C. A. Campbell as sources of this idea of freedom.

30. Ibid., 345.

31. Ibid., 343–344. My emphasis.

32. Geach, *Providence and Evil*, 5.

33. Creel, *Divine Impassibility*, 125.

34. Hick, *Evil and the God of Love*, 289–290.

35. Origen, "The First Principles," in vol. 4, *The Ante-Nicene Fathers* (Grand Rapids, Mich.: Eerdmans, 1976), Reprint of the Edinburgh Edition, 3.5.8.

36. Talbott, "The Doctrine of Everlasting Punishment," 38.

4: Hell and Divine Goodness

1. John Wesley, *Works* (Grand Rapids, Mich.: Baker, 1979; reprint of the 1872 edition), 10:227. I cite this older edition of Wesley's *Works* here and elsewhere because the New Abingdon edition (1984-), which I also cite, is at this writing still incomplete.

2. That Wesley made this claim with full seriousness is shown in his attention to God's concern for the happiness of animals, and in his belief that final redemption will include the animal kingdom. See his sermon "The General Deliverance" in *Works* (Nashville, Tenn.: Abingdon, 1985), 2:436-450.

3. It may seem that it is inconsistent to claim that God is morally good, that he is free in the libertarian sense, and that he is necessarily good. For an interesting argument that these claims are compatible, see Thomas V. Morris, "Duty and Divine Goodness," in *Anselmian Explorations* (Notre Dame, Ind.: University of Notre Dame Press, 1987), 26-41. For more on God's necessary goodness, see in the same volume "The Necessity of God's Goodness," 42-69.

4. Marilyn McCord Adams, "Duns Scotus on the Goodness of God," *Faith and Philosophy* 4 (1987): 487.

5. 1 John 4:19.

6. According to Molinism, a person's state at death is decisive for eternity. If one is in a state of grace at death he is saved, otherwise he is not.

7. Russell, *Why I Am Not a Christian*, 35.

8. Molina believed that God spares some persons by removing them by premature death before they fall into mortal sin. This seems to be the point of Wisdom 4:11, which Molina cites as scriptural evidence for middle knowledge. See *On Divine Foreknowledge* (Part IV of the Concordia), qu. 14, art. 13, disp. 49, no. 9.

9. Wesley, *Works* (1872), 10:235; cf. *Works* (1985), 2:540-541.

10. *Works* (1985), 2:582-583. Wesley's insistence that "without holiness no man shall see the Lord" points up that he did not have a superficial conception of happiness. Indeed, he often linked the two notions together, holding that "it is not possible in the nature of things that a man should be happy who is not holy." *Works* (1985), 2:195. See also 1:251, 411; 2:431; 4:300-301.

11. This involves, of course, some sort of idea of purgatory. Stripped of certain fanciful notions which have become associated with the doctrine, it plays an important role in some Protestant, as well as Catholic, theology. For a good summary of recent Protestant accounts of the

doctrine, see Hick, *Evil and the God of Love*, 345-348. See also John Lawson, *Introduction to Christian Doctrine* (Grand Rapids, Mich.: Francis Asbury Press of Zondervan, 1980), 261-263; C. S. Lewis, *The Great Divorce* (New York: Macmillan, 1946), 67-69.

12. This would involve, among other things, resources for the healing of psychological and emotional damage which hinder a favorable response to God. A rejection of God which was rooted in (innocently acquired) psychological damage would not be a decisive rejection of God. Indeed, it would not be a rejection of God at all, but only a negative reaction to a badly distorted picture of God. For a pastorally sensitive account of how emotional damage distorts one's concept of God and affects one's response to him, see David A. Seamands, *Healing of Memories* (Wheaton, Ill.: Victor Books, 1985), 95-122. See also C. S. Lewis's suggestive discussion of "Morality and Psychoanalysis" in *Mere Christianity* (New York: Macmillan, 1943), 83-87.

13. It may be the case that Wesley believed something like this, at least implicitly. For he maintained in some of his other writings that no one had the right to assume all the heathen were damned. Rather, we should leave their fate up to God, who loves all creatures. See *Works* (1986), 3:295-296, 494-495. In another sermon, Wesley argued that the problem of evil could be resolved only in the belief that the gospel will be spread throughout the whole world. He remarked in that sermon that God has "a thousand ways to foolish man unknown" of getting the gospel to those who haven't heard. "And," Wesley added, "he surely will." *Works* (1985), 2:497.

14. William Lane Craig, *The Only Wise God* (Grand Rapids, Mich.: Baker, 1987), 150-151. See also Craig, " 'No Other Name': A Middle Knowledge Perspective on the Exclusivity of Salvation Through Christ," *Faith and Philosophy* 6 (1989): 184-185.

15. Craig, "No Other Name," 184. The notion of transworld damnation, is, of course, analogous to Plantinga's notion of transworld depravity.

16. Ibid., 186.

17. Both of these claims, of course, follow from Craig's view. Craig's commitment to the latter of these creates a paradox in his position. Or so it has been argued at any rate, in a recent paper by William Hasker ("Middle Knowledge and the Damnation of the Heathen: A Response to William Craig," *Faith and Philosophy* 8 (1991): 380-389. Hasker invites us to consider the case of Parson Peter, who is contemplating going to the mission field to preach to persons who otherwise would never hear the gospel. As he ponders this decision, he wonders whether there are persons who would be saved if he goes, who would otherwise be lost. As a result of reading Craig's paper, he arrives at an affirmative answer,

drawing particular inspiration from his claim that "God has so providentially ordered things that through us the good news will be brought to persons who God knew would respond if they heard it" ("No Other Name," 186).

But then Parson Peter considers the question from another angle. Now he wonders whether, if he does not go to the mission field, there are persons who would then be lost, but who would have been saved had he taken the gospel to them. But this time, following Craig's reasoning, he arrives at a negative answer. All those persons who never hear the gospel suffer from transworld damnation, so they would not have accepted the gospel even if they had heard it. So Parson Peter has arrived at conflicting answers concerning his question of whether there are persons who would be saved if he goes to preach to them, who would otherwise be lost. Thus the paradox.

Hasker maintains that Craig can avoid the paradox only by accepting the following proposition, which, he says, "it is hard to see how any orthodox Christian could accept."

> [p] All those who accept the gospel and are saved would have been saved even if the gospel had never been preached to them (p. 386).

At first glance, it might appear that the position I have defended entails [p]. What is entailed, however, is something like the following:

> [p′] All those who accept the gospel before death in this world and are saved would accept the gospel and be saved after death if the gospel had not been preached to them in this life.

18. Richard Swinburne, *Faith and Reason* (Oxford: Clarendon, 1981), 150.

19. Calvin, *Institutes*, 3.21.6.

20. *Concordia*, qu. 14, art. 13, disp. 53, part. 3, no. 16.

21. Craig, "No Other Name," 182.

22. See Barnhart, "Theodicy and the Free Will Defence," 444.

23. In view of the argument of this section, I think we can now render a judgment on the view suggested by Hick (cited in the previous chapter) that given God's nature it is very probable that all will be saved. If the preceding argument is sound, it seems Hick's claim should be rejected. So far as God's nature is concerned, it seems to be an entirely open question whether or not all will be saved.

24. Richard Swinburne, "A Theodicy of Heaven and Hell," in *The Existence and Nature of God*, ed. Alfred J. Freddoso (Notre Dame, Ind.: University of Notre Dame, 1983), 49.

25. Cited by Creel, *Divine Impassibility*, 141.

26. For an example of the latter, see Nicholas Wolterstorff, "Suffering Love," in *Philosophy and the Christian Faith*, ed. Thomas V. Morris (Notre Dame, Ind.: University of Notre Dame Press, 1988), 196-237.

27. Geach, *Providence and Evil*, 128.

28. Creel, *Divine Impassibility*, 125-126.

29. Ibid., 134. For Creel's full discussion of the point, see 132-139.

30. Ibid., 142. See also 125; 141-143.

31. Cf. Marilyn Adams's beautifully expressed thoughts on those who may persist in resisting God's love in her essay "Separation and Reversal in Luke-Acts," in *Philosophy and the Christian Faith*, ed. Thomas V. Morris (Notre Dame, Ind.: University of Notre Dame Press), 110-115.

32. Cited by Hick in *Evil and the God of Love*, 235.

5: Hell and Human Freedom

1. Graham Greene, *The Heart of the Matter* (New York: Penguin Books, 1962), 232.

2. It may be doubted whether Scobie really represents a decisive choice of evil, since it is not clear that he rejected God in optimal conditions. In one passage with large implications, particularly in light of middle knowledge, Scobie says to himself: "If Louise [his wife] had stayed I should never have loved Helen, I would never have been blackmailed by Yusef [the unscrupulous trader], never have committed that act of despair. I would have been myself still—the same self that lay stacked in fifteen years of diaries, not this broken cast" (p. 228). So the question is whether Scobie was all along a bad man who had never been tested or a good man overwhelmed by circumstances (see pp. 245, 272).

3. *Paradise Lost*, I, 263.

4. *Paradise Lost*, IV, 108-113.

5. Swinburne, "A Theodicy of Heaven and Hell, 49.

6. Talbott, "The Doctrine of Everlasting Punishment," 37.

7. Psychiatrist M. Scott Peck refers to certain patients "who have crossed the line and descended into 'radical', likely inescapable, evil." *People of the Lie* (New York: Simon and Schuster, 1983), 47.

8. Greene, *The Heart of the Matter*, 272.

9. Talbott, "The Doctrine of Everlasting Punishment," 36.

10. John R. Silber, "Introduction" to Immanuel Kant, *Religion Within the Limits of Reason Alone* (New York: Harper and Row, 1960), cxxix. Silber refers the reader to *The Sickness Unto Death* in a footnote.

11. Kierkegaard, *The Sickness Unto Death*, 220. *The Sickness Unto Death* is preceded in the volume by *Fear and Trembling*.

12. Kierkegaard, *The Sickness Unto Death*, 154.

13. Ibid., 159-160. See also 162.

14. Ibid., 210.

15. Ibid., 147-148, 163, 182.

16. Ibid., 236.

17. Ibid., 238.

18. Ibid., 239.

19. It is noteworthy that M. Scott Peck came to this conclusion from his study of evil from a psychological standpoint. Evil people are not defined, he writes, by the magnitude of their sins. "The answer is by the consistency of their sins. While usually subtle, their destructiveness is remarkably consistent" *People of the Lie*, 71.

20. See Revelation 20:1-3.

21. Eleonore Stump, "Sanctification, Hardening of the Heart, and Frankfurt's Concept of Free Will," *Journal of Philosophy* 88 (1988): 415-416. My analysis of consistency in terms of first- and second-order desires was largely inspired by Stump's paper. Although she does not here address the doctrine of hell, she indicates that Frankfurt's account of a person and of free will may illumine the nature of hell (see p. 411). In the passage just cited, she is employing Frankfurt's account to explain how and why God hardens the hearts of some sinners. It should be added that, as in the case of Scobie, we cannot be sure that Goebbel's choice of evil described in the passage was made despite optimal grace and was therefore decisive. Perhaps he would repent, given optimal grace. His example illustrates, however, what such decisive choice would be like.

22. Swinburne, "A Theodicy of Heaven and Hell," 48-49.

23. In saying this, I am, of course, rejecting the view that it is analytically true that we always act on our strongest desire. Many times, to do what is right, we must act against our strongest desire, at least our strongest *felt* desire.

24. Thomas B. Talbott, "On the Divine Nature and the Nature of Divine Freedom," *Faith and Philosophy* 5 (1988): 13.

25. Actually, this is only a partial account of Talbott's analysis of freedom. For more detail see pp. 13-18 of the article just cited.

26. Talbott, "The Doctrine of Everlasting Punishment," 39. It is important to note that Talbott views the torment he has described as a matter of punishment of which "God himself is the author," p. 35.

27. C. S. Lewis, *The Great Divorce*, 36, emphasis added.

28. Kierkegaard, *The Sickness Unto Death*, 205-206. See also 207.

29. Luke 16:19-31.

30. It should not, however, be inferred from this that the damned do not know they are wrong. It is noteworthy that the parable concludes with Lazarus responding to the rich man that those who do not listen to Moses and the prophets will not believe even if someone rises from the

dead. This suggests that those in hell know they are wrong because they are graciously confronted afresh with the fact of their evil. Nevertheless, they do not know they are wrong with the full moral clarity of those who admit their sin and repent of it. Because they are unwilling to admit their sin, they are shaped by a lie rather than the truth. Being so shaped is of the essence of damnation.

31. Kierkegaard, *The Sickness Unto Death*, 242.

32. M. Scott Peck suggests this is true in cases he has seen "in which an individual made an evil choice for no apparent reason other than the pure desire to exercise the freedom of his or her will." See *People of the Lie*, 82.

33. Alec Kassman, "On Punishing," *Proceedings of the Aristotelian Society* 77, 231.

34. Talbott, "The Doctrine of Everlasting Punishment," 36.

35. Cf. C. S. Lewis's remark: "There may be a truth in the saying that 'hell is hell, not from its own point of view, but from the heavenly point of view.' I do not think this belies the severity of our Lord's words. It is only to the damned that their fate could ever seem less than unendurable" *The Problem of Pain*, 126. See also Eleonore Stump, "The Problem of Evil," *Faith and Philosophy* 4 (1985): 400-402; 419-420.

36. Kierkegaard, *The Sickness Unto Death*, 214. Of course, for Kierkegaard if a person "is unable to get it into his head" it is finally because he is *unwilling* to do so.

37. Of course, there are other options besides these for upholding this view. Especially worth noting is the classical idea—found in Augustine and Aquinas—that goodness and being are identical. Since the damned have being, and thereby retain some measure of goodness, it is good in God's sight that they remain in existence rather than be annihilated. See Hick, *Evil and the God of Love*, 52-53; Eleonore Stump, "Dante's Hell, Aquinas's Moral Theory, and the Love of God," *Canadian Journal of Philosophy* 16 (1986): 195-197. I agree with Hick that this represents God as taking an aesthetic rather than an ethical or personal stance toward creation. This is inadequate as an account of God's relationship to free creatures. See also Hick, pp. 193-198.

6: Hell and Human Misery

1. Matthew 8:12; 18:9. I discuss the appropriateness of describing hell as a "place" in section IV of this chapter.

2. See Mark 9:42-48, particularly verse 48. It is worth noting that in the passage just cited, Jesus is quoting from the Old Testament. See Isaiah 66:24.

3. St. Augustine, *The City of God*, trans. Marcus Dods, in *Nicene and Post-Nicene Fathers*, vol. II (Grand Rapids, Mich.: Eerdmans, 1977), Bk 21, ch. 9.

4. St. Thomas Aquinas, *Summa Theologiae*, translated by Fathers of the English Dominican Province, Supplement to Part 3, qu. 97, art. 2.

5. Wesley, *Works* (1986), 3:37. It is worth remarking that Wesley, along with the other classical theologians cited, seems to assume that personal identity includes continuity of memory as well as continuity of character. The whole issue of personal identity and immortality is, of course, a difficult one and is obviously relevant to the doctrine of hell. It is, however, subsidiary to my main concerns, and I cannot engage it in detail here without going too far afield.

6. Dante, *The Inferno*, trans. John Ciardi (New York: Mentor Books, 1954), Canto 14, 60 63.

7. John Milton, *Paradise Lost*, 4, 75. See also 4, 20-23.

8. Jonathan Edwards, *Works* (Leeds: Edward Baines, 1811), 6:488.

9. Wesley, *Works* (1986), 2:195. Emphasis added.

10. Geach, *Providence and Evil*, 138-139.

11. *Summa Theologiae*, Sup. to Part 3, qu. 98, art. 9.

12. Wesley, *Works* (1986), 3:34.

13. The lack of true friendship in hell may, however, be a direct consequence of the evil characters of the damned, as I argue below.

14. *Summa Theologiae*, Sup. to Part 3, qu. 97, art. 4.

15. *Summa Theologiae*, Sup. to Part 3, qu. 97, art. 5.

16. John Calvin, *Commentary on a Harmony of the Evangelists*, trans. William Pringle (Grand Rapids, Mich.: Eerdmans, 1949), vol. I, 201. See also Calvin's *Institutes*, 3, 25, 12.

17. Geach, *Providence and Evil*, 146. Geach does not cite the passage in Edwards which he has in mind. See, however, Edwards, *Works*, 6:492.

18. Wesley, *Works* (1986), 3:40-41.

19. Edwards, *Works*, 4:516.

20. Stump, "Dante's Hell, Aquinas's Moral Theory, and the Love of God," 197.

21. C. S. Lewis, *The Great Divorce*, 18-21.

22. *Summa Theologiae*, Sup. to Part 3, qu. 98, art. 7.

23. *The City of God*, Bk. 21, chaps. 3, 8.

24. *Summa Theologiae*, Sup. to Part 3, qu. 86, art. 3.

25. Wesley, *Works* (1986), 3:41. Wesley also suggests that the laws of nature may be changed to prevent those cast into the fires of hell from being consumed. See p. 38.

26. Edwards, *Works*, 7:497.

27. St. Thomas Aquinas, *Summa Contra Gentiles*, trans. Vernon J. Bourke, Book 3, Part II, ch. 145. Aquinas goes on to quote Psalm 10:7 as well. For a similar argument for the idea that hell shall include punishment from other elements of the natural order, see *Summa Theologiae*, Sup. to Part 3, qu. 97, art. 1.

28. *Summa Theologiae*, Sup. to Part 3, qu. 86, art. 3.

29. For an important discussion of some related issues, see Marilyn McCord Adams, "Hell and the God of Justice," *Religious Studies* 11 (1975): 433–447. Adams is not concerned specifically with physical punishment, but with the more general question of whether there are principles of justice which require God to punish sinners eternally. Adams assumes this punishment includes more than separation from God.

30. Geach, *Providence and Evil*, 138.

31. John 14:2.

32. Edwards, *Works*, 7:504–505. This is the sermon quoted in note 26 above.

33. Wesley, *Works* (1986), 2:19.

34. For a recent defense of the role of self-interest in moral motivation, including comment on the relevance of this to the doctrines of heaven and hell, see Basil Mitchell, *Morality: Religions and Secular* (Oxford: Clarendon Press, 1980), 138–145.

Conclusion

1. Recall Martin Marty's view (discussed in the Introduction) that belief in God no longer has a significant place in contemporary moral pedagogy since belief in hell has traditionally been part of belief in God, and the doctrine of hell is no longer culturally available. Noteworthy here is George Will's recent column entitled "Needed: A John Wesley To Teach Morals" (Lexington *Herald-Leader*, June 2, 1991) in which he argued (following Roger Starr) that many of our social ills can best be cured by "remoralizing" those who have been demoralized. If I am right, contemporary would-be Wesleys should include in their message a morally credible account of the doctrine of hell.

2. See, for example, the positive assessment of "conditional immortality" by evangelical New Testament scholar John Wenham in his *The Enigma of Evil* (Grand Rapids: Academie Books of Zondervan, 1985), 27–41. (Wenham's book was first published in 1974 by Inter-Varsity Press under the title *The Goodness of God*.) It is also noteworthy that influential evangelical author John Stott has recently written favorably about the annihilationist alternative. See "John Stott on Hell," *World Christian* (May 1988), 31–37. For a recent Roman Catholic defense of universalist exegesis, see Hans Urs Von Balthasar, *Dare We Hope "That All Men*

Be Saved"? trans. David Kipp and Lothar Krauth (San Francisco: Ignatius Press, 1988), 29-46; 177-187.

Among the philosophers, Richard Swinburne has recently suggested that annihilation may be the final fate of the wicked. See his *Responsibility and Atonement* (Oxford: Clarendon, 1989), 180-184. And Marilyn McCord Adams offers exegetical support for at least hoping for universal salvation in "Separation and Reversal in Luke-Acts," in *Philosophy and the Christian Faith*, ed. Thomas V. Morris, (Notre Dame, Ind.: University of Notre Dame Press, 1988), 92-117.

3. It is doubtful, however, whether advocates of annihilationism can claim a similar tradition. See the article "Conditional Immortality" in *The Oxford Dictionary of the Christian Church*, ed. F. L. Cross (London: Oxford University Press, 1958), 325.

INDEX

Abraham, 128
Acceptance vs. belief, 19-20
Adams, Marilyn, 84, 172 n. 31, 176 n. 29, 177 n. 2
Adams, Robert, 42-44, 50
Aionos, 12, 53
Annihilation, 4, 11, 136-138, 158, 175 n. 2, 177 n. 3
Apostles' Creed, 6
Aquinas, 58, 140-141, 143-149, 151, 163 n. 5, 164 n. 5, 166 n. 3, 174 n. 37
Aristotle, 45
Athanasian Creed, 166 n. 37
Augustine, 58, 124, 140-141, 143, 146, 163 n. 5, 166 n. 3, 174 n. 37

Baptism, 86
Barnhart, J. E., 4, 25-27, 30
Bauckham, 2, 21
Belial, 116, 130
Bellarmine, Robert, 163 n. 5
Berdyaev, Nicholas, 26
Berger, 30-31
Berkhof, Hendrikus, 22-25
Bernstein, Alan, 26
Biblical interpretation, 15, 158-159
Brasnett, Bertrand, 106

Calvin, 58, 61, 63, 99, 144
Calvinism, 13, 35-37, 41, 58-70, 80-81, 164 n. 5, 166 n. 3
Campbell, C. A., 168 n. 29
Capaneus, 142
Character, moral, 128, 130-131, 134
Christ, Jesus, 5-6, 9, 11, 14, 22, 25, 27-29, 39, 53-54, 65, 97-98, 127-128, 139

Christian heart, witness of, 18-22, 26
Circumstances, 87, 91
Conscience, 141
Consistency of evil, 120, 122-124, 128, 173 n. 19
Convinced universalist view, 14, 54, 162 n. 32
Counterfactuals of freedom, 38, 40-44
Craig, William Lane, 96-97, 101, 170 n. 17
Cultural availability, 8-9
Cyprian, 163 n. 5

Dante, 142, 174 n. 37
David, 43
Decisive choice of evil, 115-117, 120-121, 124, 126, 136, 138
Decisive response to grace, 89-90
Deprivation, 143
DeRivo, Peter, 45
Descartes, 20
Desires, 120-121, 123, 134, 173 n. 23
Despair, 118-119, 128
Divine attributes, 15, 33, 85
Double effect, principle of, 34, 37, 166 n. 34
Duthie, Charles, 18-19, 21-22, 26

Ecumenical councils, 54
Edwards, Jonathan, 1, 3, 58, 142, 144-147, 151, 154, 163 n. 10, 166 n. 3
Effectual Call, 59-60, 63
Enablement, 60-62, 66-67
Erasmus, 91-92
Evil, problem of, 3-5, 71-73, 77-78, 170 n. 13

False hope, 2
Farrar, F. W., 10-13, 53
Fathers, church, 54, 158
Feasible worlds, 73, 91, 101
Feuerbach, Ludwig, 26
Feuerbachian arguments, 27, 30
Fire, 139-142, 144-149, 151, 166 n. 37
Flew, Anthony, 65
Flint, Thomas, 63, 73, 164 n. 5, 166 nn. 2, 16
Foreknowledge: absolute/infallible, 34-35, 39, 44, 47, 52, 54, 85, 93, 113; based on present tendencies, 45-46, 49; Calvinistic view of, 35-37, 45; Compatibility with freedom, 34, 39, 47; General, 46-53, 74-77, 85, 93, 103-105; independent of human choice, 36; and intention, 33-34, 36, 40-41, 49, 52, 164n. 2; Molinist view, 39-41
Frankfurt, Harry, 173 n. 21
Freddoso, Alfred, 4, 165 nn. 14-15, 166 n. 2
Freedom, 12, 15, 38, 107, 116, 134, 136, 138; compatilist, 39, 64-68, 79, 81, 113; libertarion, 34, 36, 39, 60-70, 80-81, 113, 125, 133, 136; moral, 129-130; overridden, 104-105, 132, 134-135
Free Will Defense, 40, 72-73, 96
Frustration, God's, 74-76
Future contingents, 37, 40-41, 44-46, 74

Gallup poll, 3
Geach, Peter, 6, 8-9, 29, 45-46, 57, 75, 106, 143, 144, 148, 150, 163 n. 5
Genetic fallacy, 27, 30
Goodness: as love, 83-84; necessary, 83, 98; perfect, 83
Grand Master of Chess, 45, 49
Great Divorce, The, 13, 123
Greene, Graham, 114, 117

Happiness: God's, 109-110; Human, 84, 87, 93, 104-105, 108, 124-126, 128, 130-133, 150, 169 n. 10
Hartshorne, Charles, 168
Hasker, William, 170 n. 17
Heart of the Matter, The, 144
Heathen, 11

Heaven, 125-126, 128-129, 137-138
"Hell Disappeared. No One Noticed. A Civic Argument," 7
Hick, John, 13, 70-80, 163 n. 10, 170 n. 11, 171 nn. 11, 23, 174 n. 37
Hitler, A., 121-122
Holiness, 10, 88, 169 n. 10
Holy Spirit, 11, 18-19, 21, 24, 60, 133
Hopeful Universalist View, 13
Hume, David, 3, 9

Illusion, 125, 131-133
Immorality of Hell, alleged, 15, 29
Impassibility, 106
Incarnation, 6, 28, 53-54, 98
Isolation, 145, 152

Jonah, 48

Kant, I., 117, 122, 125
Kantian arguments, 154-155
Kassman, Alec, 132
Kaufman, Gordon, 162 n. 20
Keilah, 43
Kenny, Anthony, 45
Kierkegaard, Søren, 24-25, 117-119, 122, 127-128, 137-138, 143, 151

Lawson, John, 170 n. 11
Lazarus, 127, 173 n. 30
Leibniz, Gottfried, 4
Lewis, C. S., 13, 123, 126, 145, 151, 163 n. 4, 170 nn. 11-12
Lombard, Peter, 163 n. 5
Luther, Martin, 58, 91-92

Mackie, J. L., 71-72
Mann, Arthur, 8
Marty, Martin, 7-9, 162 n. 23, 176 n, 1
Middle Knowledge, 37-44, 50, 73, 80, 85, 101, 105, 172 n. 2
Mill, James, 5, 33
Mill, John Stuart, 5, 8-9, 33-34, 36, 49, 52
Miller, Richard B., 27
Milton, John, 115, 122, 142
Missions, 94-95, 97
Mitchell, Basil, 176 n. 34
Modified Orthodox View (of Hell), 13, 54

Molina, Luis de, 37-40, 42, 99
Molinism, 37-44, 85-93, 96-97, 100-101
Morally sensitive belief in Hell, 30-31
Moral Pedagogy, 7, 157, 176 n. 1
Morris, Thomas V., 48, 164 n. 16, 169 n. 3
Mossner, E. C., 3-4
Mystery, 88

Napolean, 122
Nero, 153
Nicene Creed, 6
Nietzsche, Friedrich, 106

Optimal Grace, 88-90, 97-98, 100-102, 131, 137, and adversity, 89; and divine freedom, 98-100; decisive response to, 89-90, 93-94, 97, 103-104; offered beyond death, 92-94, 100; and self-deception, 131
Origen, 80
Otte, Richard, 44

Paradise Lost, 115
Paul, St., 117
Peck, Scott, 172 n. 7, 173 n. 19, 174 n. 32
Personal identity, 135, 175 n. 5
Perversity, 129
Pinnock, Clark, 168 n. 19
Place, Hell as, 152-153
Plantinga, Alvin, 40-41, 72-73, 96, 163 n. 3
Plato, 117
Possible worlds, 72-73, 168 n. 25
Power to act, 124, 132-133; vs. psychological possibility, 124, 130, 132-133
Prayer, public schools, 7
Predestination: Calvinist view, 36, 59; Molinist view, 37-39
Process Thought, 106, 136
Proportion of damned, 102-104
Punishment, divine, 7, 10, 12-14, 22, 26, 31, 39, 173 n. 26, 176 n. 29
Purgatory, 169 n. 11
Purification, Hell as, 14, 22
Puritans, 8
Pusey, E. B., 10-12, 53-54

Quinn, Philip, 168 n. 19

Real belief in Hell, 31
Resurrection, 152
Revelation, 27, 29, 53, 87
Russell, Bertrand, 2, 5, 8-9, 28-29, 86

Salvation, 6-7, 57, 84, 92-94, 98, 114
Satan, 115, 122, 125, 142
Saul, 43
Schleiermacher, Friedrich, 110
Scobie, 114-115, 117, 122, 172 n. 2
Seamands, David, 170 n. 12
Self, becoming a, 118
Self-deception, 129-131, 133, 138
Self-interest, 155, 176 n. 34
Short, Robert, 4
Signals of transcendance, 30
Silber, John, 117, 122
Sin, 118-120, 124-125, 128, 130, 132-133, 144, 154-155
"Sinners in the Hands of an Angry God," 1, 163 n. 10
Skyscraper analogy, 51
Sorrow, Divine, 77, 106-107, 109-110
Starr, Roger, 176 n. 1
Stump, Eleanore, 121, 145, 174 nn. 35, 37
Suffering: Physical, 139, 141, 144-149, 151-152; Spiritual, 141-142, 150
Suicide, 135-137
Swinburne, Richard, 47-49, 98, 105, 115, 123, 134, 177 n. 2
Systematic Theology, 15

Talbott, Thomas, 14, 80, 105, 115, 117, 124-125, 130-132, 135
Tertullian, 163 n. 5
Traditional Calvinist view of Hell, 13
Traditional Orthodox view of Hell, 13
Traditional popular view of Hell, 12
Transworld damnation, 96-97, 170 n. 15
Trinity, 6

Unintelligibility of Hell, alleged, 15, 113-114
Universalism, 3, 6, 11-12, 18-19, 22, 53-54, 58, 71, 74, 79-81, 131-132, 158

"Usefullness of Sin," 3
"Utility of Religion," 5

Vatican II, 8
Vindictiveness, 25-29
Von Balthasar, Hans Urs, 176 n. 2

Warden, Rev. John, 3
Wenham, John, 176 n. 2
Wesley, John, 25, 60, 62, 64, 83-84,
    87-91, 110, 141-142, 144-146,
    150, 153, 155, 170 n. 13, 176 n. 1
Westminster Confession, 35, 58
Westminster Divines, 68-70
Will, George, 176 n. 1